HEROIN:
THE RIPPLE EFFECT

TIM WEBER

AuthorHouse™
1663 Liberty Drive
Bloomington, IN 47403
www.authorhouse.com
Phone: 833-262-8899

Scripture quotations marked NIV are taken from the Holy Bible, New International Version®. NIV®. Copyright © 1973, 1978, 1984 by International Bible Society. Used by permission of Zondervan. All rights reserved. [Biblica]

Published by AuthorHouse 11/16/2021

ISBN: 978-1-6655-4216-6 (sc)
ISBN: 978-1-6655-4528-0 (hc)
ISBN: 978-1-6655-4215-9 (e)

Library of Congress Control Number: 2021921694

Print information available on the last page.

This book is printed on acid-free paper.

Dedication

This book is in memory and honor of my friend, George Butler, whose connection to me allowed me to become who I am today. George is the person who introduced me to the many people in my hometown who helped to pave the path to start the addiction prevention work that I hold so passionately and so dear.

When I first met George, he was a drug investigator with the Carroll County State's Attorney's office. He was also a "Choices" instructor for at-risk teenagers, when we first met. Our friendship grew and lasted until his last day on this earth.

We met when I had five years of sobriety under my belt. He never missed attending my sober anniversary events. Without question, my connection with George put me in a position to help many other people.

George passed away on August 13, 2020. Rest in peace, my dear friend.

I am also dedicating this book to another very special person in my life. His name is Isiah Robertson. I spent almost two and a half years with Isiah, the owner of a drug rehabilitation program which I went through a couple of times.

That experience was where my love of helping others started. Isiah taught me that, as he said, "some of us need to do this kind of service to others, 24/7." We need to live what we say, we need to immerse ourselves with helping others, in my view.

On December 6, 2019, Isiah died in a car crash after he left an event where he was speaking with a group of high school football players. He died after doing what he loved—helping others by sharing a message of hope.

Ironically, Isiah died on the very same calendar date that my mother died. She actually died forty years earlier on that day of the year.

It's ironic that two of the most influential people of my life share the same anniversary date of their death.

When I attended Isiah's funeral, I was able to see the tangible evidence of the ripple effect from everyone who attended his funeral.

This is why I hope to carry forward that same ripple effect throughout my life and throughout this book.

As you read each chapter of this book, you will notice both a positive and a negative ripple effect which heroin has left behind in the lives of many. My hope is that you can understand the positive ripple effect that my relationship with Isiah had on me and everyone with whom I interact.

As you read each chapter, you can see the same ripple effect weaving throughout the lives of countless other people in recovery. So, for that gift of the positive ripple effect, George and Isiah, I am more grateful than you can imagine.

He lifted me out of the slimy pit, out of
The mud and mire; he set my feet on a rock
And gave me a firm place to stand.
—Psalm 40:2

Contents

Part 1: What It Was Like

Part 2: What Happened to Change Me

Part 3: What It Is Like Today

Part 4: The Story of the Weber Sober Homes

Part 5: The Ripple Effect Comes Full Circle

This book includes the 1st two editions of Gutters & Roses

All proceeds go to Heroin: The Ripple Effect Foundation

Foreword to the First Edition

Over the last thirty years, I have personally seen how drugs affect individuals, families, and communities. Working the streets as an undercover Maryland state police narcotics officer and then as a Carroll County drug investigator, I have worked closely with the school system; juvenile services; drug treatment court; diversion programs such as Choices, Community Conference, Heroin Action Coalition; and other support groups. This is where the author's and my paths crossed.

My first impression of Tim was of his sincerity in helping anyone involved with alcohol or drugs. He was a recovering addict with close to five years of clean time. He was literally on the street as a "junkie", but was able to rise above, mend his relationships with his family, and become a successful member of society. He speaks of his life experiences in an attempt to keep other young people from walking in his shoes. His story is quite profound and will give the reader an eye-opening picture of what it is like to be addicted to drugs. His story also gives hope that it is possible to make changes and turn your life around; he is a walking testament to that. It took years of living on the street and several near-death experiences before he decided to do what he needed to do to break the chain of addiction.

This is a must-read for anyone wanting to understand the tribulations of addiction. Whether you yourself are struggling or are in recovery or are an enabler, a family member, or even a child of an addict, the author relates to all. This book is G-rated and suitable for all ages. Tim uses his candid recollection to depict what his life was like while he was suffering from a drug addiction and ultimately how many people he affected. He is one of the lucky ones and has chosen to share his story to help others. You will find his honesty and insight insurmountable.

George A. Butler
Drug Investigator
Carroll County State's Attorney's Office

Foreword to the Second Edition

Sometimes, life takes an odd turn and we end up somewhere totally unexpected, not in the plan. Often, that is when we cross paths with the people who have the most impact on our lives. I previously worked in the religious education field at a parochial school, and Tim was an addict. I ended up in the substance abuse prevention field, and Tim was in recovery. Our paths crossed many years ago when Tim and I were both working toward a common goal of helping heroin addicts and their families.

The Substance Abuse Prevention Office combined forces with Tim and the members of the Weber Sober Homes on drug education outreach and substance abuse awareness programs, including outreach to and education of parents, students, and communities. The reach is far beyond Carroll County, as Tim has been a keynote speaker at many state events. Because of Tim's commitment and dedication, he has received the Risky Business Prevention Award for the innovative way he reaches out to youth and community. Knowing Tim has not only enriched my personal and professional life, but it has also given me deep understanding of the addictive process and recovery. Through this insight and collaboration with Tim, we offer comprehensive services of the fullest capacity to the community.

For whatever reason, Tim had to go through what he experienced in his life to become the person he is today: a compass for the lost and misguided, an instructor in faith, and a healer of the souls inflicted with the disease of addiction. Tim helps people find the lives they lost along the way. If you want a closer look into reality, you don't have to watch reality TV. Just read *Gutters & Roses: With Notes from a Sober Home*. It is the next chapter of Tim Weber's life, and it shows the remarkable difference one man is making. It is a book of courage, hope, and strength.

Linda Auerback, CPP, ICPS, Substance Abuse Prevention Supervisor
Carroll County Health Department
Bureau of Prevention, Wellness, and Recovery

Foreword to the Third Edition, from Brian DeLeonardo, Carroll County State's Attorney

The first time I met Tim Weber was in the winter of 2013. I was in the midst of my campaign to be State's Attorney for Carroll County, and my central message was that the State's Attorney was not doing anything to address the increasing appearance of heroin in our community. I was advocating for a significant, increased role in the use of treatment efforts for those addicted, as well as for the State's Attorney's Office to take a much more intensive role in prevention efforts in order to stem this rising tide.

At that time, I actually worked as a defense attorney, and had seen an increasing number of clients using heroin and tragically, some even losing their lives in the process. During my campaign, I began talking to parents, treatment providers, and some law enforcement officials who I found shared my concern over this trend. Some also saw those around them lose their lives to addiction. Even so, during that time period it was not talked about openly very often in the community and I often described the growing use of heroin as the County's "dirty little secret." It was during this time that one of the individuals who shared my concern told me "You have to meet this guy Tim Weber, as I think he could be helpful for what you want to do."

So, one weekday evening I took that advice and went to a community presentation that Tim was involved in, where there were about a dozen people in attendance. I heard Tim share his story of addiction, of his times overdosing, and how he was working now to help others out of this darkness through education and by providing peer support in his sober houses. While Tim's story was incredibly riveting, what was most apparent to me that night was his incredible passion for helping others to find a way out of their addiction. Moreover, I could see the most important commodity he was offering to those suffering from addiction was hope. That night I knew I wanted Tim to be part of the solution for the addiction challenge we faced in the County if my campaign was successful. Indeed, what I saw was that his story could not only provide hope for those battling addiction, but also could be instrumental in changing the mindset of those in law enforcement, the courts, and county government when it came to how to best approach tackling this growing issue.

Ultimately, I was successful in my campaign effort and assumed the position of State's Attorney in January of 2015. I quickly began the plan to create a new and unique position in the State's Attorney's Office called the Drug Treatment and Education Liaison. My intent was to have this position help transform the court system and law enforcement approach to those suffering from drug dependence. What was unique about this role is that I wanted someone in long-term recovery, as it was my belief that such a person would be far more effective in working with those presently addicted. Of course, a prosecutors' office would normally not hire someone with a prior criminal record and history of overdosing, but I believed this atypical challenge we faced called for an atypical solution. Of course, I had no idea if he would ultimately want to work for my office, but without question, I created this position with Tim in mind.

After getting the necessary funding a few months later, I invited Tim to my office to discuss this newly-created role and what I believed he would be able to accomplish if he accepted my offer. I recall telling

Tim that I wanted him to do what he has been doing for the last several years—helping people with addiction and providing a message of prevention. I emphasized, however, that he would be able to have a greater impact on even more people in this new role because of what I could offer him: a "bigger megaphone" for his message by being a member of the State's Attorney's Office.

Tim agreed and for the next several years, we were able to create some tremendous initiatives that really helped at times lead the way in our State. He was able to serve as a 24/7 phone number contact for our law enforcement to call, sometimes from the side of the road, that would allow him to then take the person and get them into treatment. One police chief in our county remarked that Tim was so successful getting people into treatment in his town that there was a major reduction in thefts and burglaries that he attributed to Tim's work. Tim would sometimes text me late at night from the hospital as he waited for someone brought there after an overdose and report he was staying with them overnight until they could go to treatment the next day. He was actually able to serve as a "one-stop" resource for everyone in the county looking for treatment as he would not only know what was available, but would work to get them into treatment. Tim made it such that help was just a phone call away. It was not long before parents, police, judges, and even defense lawyers were calling for Tim's help with someone. We were also able to deliver educational programs to all of our high schools and middle schools, where the State's Attorney's Office had been silent. And, perhaps what I am most proud of is that we were able to start a vigil to remember those lost to drug addiction that yearly has reached attendance levels in excess of 400 people. I often would remark to people that Tim would still bring the same level of passion and commitment to his job even if I told him he was not getting paid because what he was doing was his calling and not just a work assignment.

Through it all, what Tim shows is that the role of those that have battled addiction and made it through to the other side is incredibly powerful in helping those currently suffering. Moreover, Tim offers a different picture to the entire community when it comes to those suffering from addiction. Police, judges, government officials, school board members, and even my own prosecutors benefitted from hearing Tim's story and seeing the overwhelming positive impact he was having on the community. After spending any time with Tim, one cannot simply dismiss those addicted as "lost causes" or "not worth the effort." Tim shows that they are worth the effort, and that each one still has a great deal of promise and value to offer the community. In his time with my office, Tim not only helped countless people battling addiction, but he helped change our county's entire mindset and approach to addiction. As Tim continues to write the next chapter in his life, he takes with him my gratitude, admiration and friendship.

Introduction

My hope is that this book will help others in the world suffering from the disease of addiction. I spent years upon years struggling with drugs and alcohol and was finally led out by the ever-loving grace of God and a 12-Step program. As you read through this book, you will despise the person I became in my active addiction, and I hope you see the depths to which we can go as addicts.

But there is a happy ending to this horrific story. I pray you will receive a message of hope and understand that it is not the person you should despise, but the disease. I know God saved me so I could tell this story to everyone. It took many years for the seed that was planted in me long ago to finally germinate and grow. Now that it has, I hope and pray I can do the same—give a message of hope and plant the seed of God in someone so he or she will, in return, pass it on to others. The recovery movement is mind-blowing in its message of hope and acceptance. This story tells how I was transformed into an advocate for others who have walked in my shoes.

I thank God for the message Isiah Robertson from the House of Isaiah gave me years ago. Isiah was the very first person who introduced me to God, and I will be forever indebted to him. It took years for that seed to grow, but it is growing daily because of the message God allowed me to hear from my friend. The most important friend you will ever have is the person who introduces you to God!

Tim Weber

Poems I Wrote
While in Jail

Under the Bridge

I used to drive across this bridge in my car;
God, if I had only known drugs would take me this far.

It was under this bridge that I drew blood red;
all the faces around me all looked dead.

An old woman sipping and nursing her wine,

how did you end up in this homeless shrine?

The smell and stench were more than I could bear.
If I could only get one more fix, I could mask my despair.

The night finally came, and I was thrown in jail.
There I was, all alone in my cell.

I dropped to my knees and cried to the Lord;

He answered me back and sent me a sword.

I read through the book and prayed once again.
Just open your heart and let me back in!

Lost in the Game

I was on my own and lost in the game; my life was filled
with sorrow and shame.

The biggest fear I had every day was that someone
would find me and take me away.

The biggest hope I had every day was that someone
would find me and take me away.

I lived on the streets with so much fear, but
this is something no one could hear.

I look at the people living their lives, going
to work, and hugging their wives.

God, I wish I could get out of this game and shed this
life of sorrow and shame!

I know there was a time when I could enjoy life and smile, but now
there is no way with all this denial.

The day finally came, and I had a touch from above; it was
sent to me in a message of love.

Now I am not on my own or lost in the game, because
I have been saved in Jesus's name!

Part 1
What It Was Like

The Mom I Barely Knew

It was December 6, 1976 at about 8:30 in the morning. I was eleven at the time and most definitely a mama's boy. I walked into my room, where my mother was sleeping. She had slept in my bed because she and my dad fought the night before. The night of the fight was just like many before. My dad had screamed and yelled at Mom; to this day I still don't know what it was about. I just know it happened a lot. Anyway, as I was going through my sock drawer I noticed my brother Pat sitting on the bed next to my mom. He looked at me and said, "Mom's not breathing."

I stared at him in disbelief. He screamed, "Go get Dad."

I ran to my dad's room, banged on the door, and in a panic screamed, "Mom is dead!"

He flew out of the shower, and dripping wet, ran to my room. He shook her and shook her. He then picked up the phone and called 911. "I need an ambulance, at…" I do remember he could not even remember our address. He was most definitely in shock. The next few minutes I really don't remember. I just know I was told to leave the room and go to the living room. Minutes later, there was an ambulance at our door and EMTs were rushing back to my room.

I must have been in a trance. I remember this part like it was yesterday. I sat in my dad's recliner with my dog, Oreo. Dogs are smart, and even he knew I needed him in my lap, just looking up at me and licking my face. In his own way he was taking care of me. I just watched all the activity in my house. I do not remember shedding one tear at that time. We loaded up and went to the Picayune Memorial Hospital. At the time we were living in Picayune, Mississippi.

I remember sitting in the waiting room and wondering what in the world was going on. Then a grim-faced doctor came out and said, "She is gone. I am sorry, sir." I think he said she had been dead on arrival.

I watched my dad and Pat closely and don't really remember any of us crying. I could be wrong, but as I recall, that is the way it was. I guess we were all in shock.

My brother Mike was off at college, so we had to drive to his school and break the news to him. I remember walking down the corridor to his dorm room. I was a few steps behind Pat and he behind Dad. All I remember is the look on Mike's face. He knew something was wrong. Why else would we all be there in the middle of the week? I didn't hear what Dad said. I just saw Mike collapse into Dad's arms and start sobbing. That is the first time I remember crying about my mom's death at all. It was like, *Okay, Mike is, so I can too.* I don't know where that came from, but that was how I felt. Mike was my idol.

So we all got in the car and drove back home. I remember thinking all the way back home, *What am I going to do?* Just last night I had taken my mom a glass of water, and she had told me she loved me, and I had said, "I love you too." And now she was dead! How could this happen? I was eleven years old and had just lost my one and only emotional caretaker—my mom! I was lost and scared and felt all alone.

The funeral was at a big church. I don't recall the name. I remember my mom had really gotten into church months before she died. Looking back now it gives me a good feeling to know she was a Christian. I only recall three things about the funeral. First, there were a lot of people I did not know. Second, my dad had one tear roll down his face, and he was gritting his teeth as if trying to hold back any emotion. It was never verbally told to me, but this is when I must have learned to show no emotion (unless of course, it was rage, which I learned very well). It was basically not allowed in my family.

Lastly, I remember my dad sitting Pat, Mike, and me on the bed at our house after the funeral and saying, "Well, boys, it is just going to be us from now on."

The Dad I Feared

Now I must go back to the few years I had with my mom and dad together. Let's just say it was not too good from what I remember. I was very young, and I know my mom was sick with arthritis. My dad was a very scary man as I recollect it. I remember countless nights of screaming and yelling coming from the living room. I would cower between my two brothers, shaking and crying. My oldest brother, Mike, would always comfort me and say everything would be okay. But as a scared little boy, all I knew was that my mom was in trouble out in the other room. And when was it going to start on one of us? This feeling of anxiety has stayed with me through my whole life.

My dad was an excellent provider and took very good care of us financially. So, this part of my story is hard to write for fear of the hurt it could cause him. However, I feel it needs to be told to get the true understanding of what my life was like through my eyes as a child. Ironically, my dad had a whole set of his own issues, which most definitely impacted my mom and us boys. He ruled the home with an iron fist. Believe it or not, today, my dad and I have reached a deeper understanding and acceptance of each other to the point that I look to him for advice and guidance in my life. We have forgiven and forgotten. I cherish our relationship today.

But my younger years were not so sweet. So here goes. Point blank, I was scared to death of my dad. I watched him beat my brother for using drugs. The night it happened I remember sitting on our couch and watching television in Houston when Mike came in from somewhere. He sat down for a minute or two. He was drinking a Dr. Pepper (he was always drinking Dr. Pepper). He then said good night to us all and went back to his room.

Minutes later, my dad followed him, and shortly after that he called Mom, Pat, and me to come watch him beat the living heck out of Mike. Then he looked at us and said, "This is what is going to happened to any of you who use drugs!"

I remember my mom trying to jump on him and stop him, but he just pushed her away. I can't tell you what was going on in my mind at that time, but even as I write it now, I can see it in color! I was probably six or seven at the time. Those were my formative years and my foundation in life was centered in fear.

Another time he caught my brother Pat smoking. My dad made him eat a whole pack of cigarettes! The sad thing was they weren't Pat's. They belonged to a neighborhood friend. Pat did smoke, but these just weren't his. And then we all went out to eat at a pizza place right after that like nothing happened. The denial was unreal!

My dad demanded respect! It was a must in our house to say, "Yes, sir" or "No, sir." And trust me, you did not want to lie to him or even come close to disrespecting him. One time, I had some friends over from next door. We were playing late one night and probably being too loud in the living room, and my dad was in one of those moods. Well, he came out and yanked me up by my underwear, and it scared me so much that I wet myself. I was maybe five or six years old, and I still remember that night. I can't tell you the embarrassment I felt in front of those two friends. I wish those memories would just disappear—but they won't.

I can say this: my father loves his three boys. And he did the best he could. After the death of my mom, things got better. He was still tough and led the house with an iron fist. But he was, I am sure, scared and wondering how in the world he was going to raise three boys on his own. But he did the best he could at the time, and times were different back then. He thought if we feared him, we would respect him and do well. And he has all the respect in the world from me! He taught me some of my most valuable assets today: honesty and one heck of a work ethic. I don't think I have ever heard my father tell a lie.

Now let me tell you another sobering truth. If there's one thing I've learned in working with people who are addicted it's that many have had some form of trauma in life. That's not to say that everyone with early childhood trauma becomes an addict. But those with addiction commonly started life experiencing trauma.

You're Not My Mom

Not too long after Mom died, Arlene came into my life. She was my dad's girlfriend, and let me tell you, she paid for it. I was the youngest of the three boys, and I gave her the most grief. She was not my mom, and I let her know every day that she was no part of our family. After all, six months earlier my dad told me it was going to be just us four now. And that didn't include some woman trying to interfere with that. She did not want to take the place of my mom, but being Dad's girlfriend and eventually moving in with us, she had no choice. Whether she wanted it or not, in my eyes she was an evil stepmother! I found out years later that she and my dad had an affair before my mom died, and that just made things worse. I hated her with a passion.

Here it is, almost four decades later, and I could not be prouder to call Arlene my mom. How this woman stuck it out with my dad, and the three of us and our addictions, still amazes me. She is one of the most precious people in my life today. I love her dearly and value her not only as a mother, but also as a very good friend.

The Addiction Begins

This is where my story leads to a point in my life when I learned to not feel and to stuff every emotion humanly possible deep down inside. This is a trait of mine that fed the desire to quiet the pain I was feeling by using drugs—and it worked.

I can tell you I don't remember my first drink, but I remember my first "drunk" like it was yesterday.

I know there were times before eight years old when I had taken sips of beer and wine at family functions or at my father's company picnics. But it meant nothing because I never drank enough to feel any effects of the alcohol. But that all changed the summer before the ninth grade when I was invited to a party with some older kids who were already in high school. Well, they had a lot of beer and weed. I don't remember smoking any weed, but I sure remember the beer.

I thought I had found the answer I had been looking for all of my short life. It made me everything I thought I wanted to be and, most importantly, everything I thought everyone else wanted me to be. I was no longer shy, timid, and afraid, and I flat out thought I could do anything that night. That feeling of power crushed the usual feeling of powerlessness I always felt, and that in turn, felt good to me.

I was accepted into a new class of people, the cool older people. Little did I know that the first feeling of being drunk would eventually lead me down a road of destruction to living under bridges and in abandoned houses.

I remember waking up the next morning with my head spinning. I threw up and felt like my head had been hit by a Mack truck. However, I could not wait to do it again as soon as possible. And I did it many times after that with the same effect of pleasure and then pain. Was this going to be the new theme of my life? Unfortunately, yes.

The cycle of pleasure and pain continued all summer long. Then the school year started, and I attended my first high school—Wilde Lake High School. I played football and met new people, and life was good—so I thought.

One day a guy in school had some Quaaludes. I think his dad was a doctor or something. Well, I bought a couple and instead of waiting until after school, I took mine right away. Thirty minutes later I was out of control. I couldn't walk, and needless to say I found myself in the office, waiting for someone to pick me up. I don't remember much about the ride home, but I do remember waking up and my dad standing over me. As you can imagine, I was pretty scared of what he was going to do. Well, there was no butt-kicking. It was worse.

He looked at me square in the eye and said, "Do you know that is how your mother died? From an overdose of pills!"

This sent me into a whirlwind of emotions from that point on about everything. I convinced myself that Mom had killed herself because she couldn't take my dad or us three boys anymore. So, there I was thirteen, already suspended from school, and we hadn't even had our first football game. And it did not end there at Wilde Lake High.

Two weeks after I returned to school, someone had some purple microdots (LSD), and once again I got some and couldn't wait until after school to do mine. We were having testing at school that day, the one where you fill in the multiple-choice dots. The acid kicked in, and I was once again out of control. I could not stop laughing in class, so I was sent to the office. They could not tell what I had done because other than my pupils being quite dilated, I seemed fine, just a little too happy. They sent me to the nurse's station to either wait for the police to come or my dad. To be honest, at that time I would have preferred the police!

About an hour went by, and a couple of friends walked by the nurse's station and looked in on me when the nurse walked out for a minute. They both said, "Dude, you better get out of here, just leave and tell them you don't know what was wrong with you and then come back tomorrow."

I think they thought that if the school found out I was on acid, I would tell who I had gotten it from or get in a lot of trouble. In any case, I scooted out of school unnoticed and walked around the lake for hours, hoping the drugs would wear off and I could go home and no one would know. Wrong! I walked through the doors of my house, and Dad and Arlene were sitting at the kitchen table, waiting for me. But to my surprise I didn't get my head caved in. It was just a look of disappointment and shame—a look I grew to know very well in the years to come. We talked for hours, and to be honest I don't know what was said. I was still tripping on the acid, and their faces were melting right before my eyes. I am not trying to glamorize that in any way. It is just the truth.

The next day, I got the news that I was expelled from school, and that meant no going back to Wilde Lake High School. Before I crawled out of bed that morning, I was listening to 98 Rock radio station and heard the breaking news: "John Lennon has been shot and killed outside his apartment." I don't know why I remember this. It is not like I was a big Beatles fan. I just remember the morning and thinking that news didn't seem nearly as bad as mine. I was already a self-centered addict.

The Move to Centennial High School

Somehow my dad got me enrolled in another high school. We happened to have just moved into another Maryland school district—Centennial High School. I was not happy about this to say the least. All my friends were at Wilde Lake, and now I had to go to another school with this big stigma attached to me. I was the kid who flipped out on drugs at Wilde Lake. Well, it didn't take me long to get a new stigma—"The Boxer," the kid who would fight anyone.

When I was twelve years old, my brother Mike took me to see the movie *Rocky*. I fell in love with boxing. I started in Slidell, Louisiana, where we moved a few months after my mom died. I started out at ninety-five pounds and was in a lot of fights in the Slidell and New Orleans areas. When we moved to Maryland, I got out of it for a year or so until I found a boxing club in Catonsville, Maryland. I had a few fights around there and a few write-ups in the paper and was known as Tim "The Boxer" or Tex's little brother. That was the nickname of my middle brother, Pat, since we were originally from Texas, where he was very well-known for his fights in school and at parties around the area. The funny thing was that we had this reputation and when people would see us, they would say, "Those are the tough guys? They can't weigh 140 pounds soaking wet!"

Okay, back to school. I guess I am saying I could use my fists very well and was always more than a little eager to show this skill off at school. I was in school for maybe one week, and someone said something to me they shouldn't have. So out the wood shop door we went. I unloaded some combinations on him, and he bled severely from the nose.

I found out later he was a diabetic and bled easily. Of course, I felt bad about this for many years. Ironically, I ended up becoming close friends with his sister throughout high school. Years later, I saw his sister at our flower shop as a customer, and she told me her brother had died. So, we made the flower arrangements for his funeral.

Nonetheless, back in high school, my immature self said that he had started the conflict. He had raised his hands, and to me that meant hit or be hit. Anyway, it was the talk of the school, and there you go. I had a new reputation I was proud of. All the time deep down inside I was scared of my own shadow. I just figured if I could take a punch from my dad and not fight back, I could fight back and no one could beat me up. Let me tell you, I found out on a number of occasions that philosophy was off. I got my share of the worst in many fights through the years. And of course, I will never forget my encounter with the diabetic boy, which haunts me to this day.

Well, the very next day the administrator of the school got wind of it, and there I was in an office, in trouble again. Thank God this man had us shake hands and promise not to take it any further. I agreed, and I thought that was that. Then he asked the other kid to go back to class. He wanted to talk to me alone.

These are the words I remember: "I understand you are a pretty good boxer, so let me ask you this. Why did you feel the need to beat the heck out of someone who couldn't fight his way out of a wet paper bag?"

In my defense, at this time I was fighting in the 139-pound weight class and was maybe five feet eight. This guy was at least six feet tall. Okay, maybe he was skinny, but he ran his mouth to the wrong new kid. I didn't say all that, but I was thinking it.

"Mr. Weber, here is your warning," said the principal. "You get in another fight and you will be expelled from my school too. I don't care if someone calls you every name in the book or raises his or her hand to you. You come to me, and I will deal with it." A positive role model relationship was born that day—tough, yet supportive.

The funny thing is that this man and I became close. I had a couple of situations come up that year, and I actually went to him and told him. No names of course, but I at least got it out there. He always followed my fights and was supposed to come to a couple of them but never made it to any. I found out just recently from someone I met through my business that he passed away years ago.

So, life went on at Centennial. I met and got close to many people. A few I have to mention are Joey, Rick, Kurt, and James. We called ourselves "The Boys." We did everything together. Joey and I were the closest. He actually went to Atholton High School and was a state champion golfer, for I think two years in a row. Man, I loved Joey! The reason I say *loved* in the past tense is because he died of this disease several years ago. I was devastated, but I was already so far gone in my own addiction that I couldn't even make it to his funeral. I will get to that later.

Let me just say that when you saw Joey, you saw me and vice versa—always. He lived with me for a while during high school. God, I miss him. I know he would be so proud of me for being clean! Anyway, we all had fake IDs, and let me tell you, we did all our college partying in high school. We went to Coast to Coast (a bar) for "Drink and Drown Night" every Thursday from eleventh grade all the way through the twelfth. We would always have a bong, a bag of weed, and brews every weekend and throughout the week. We have always partied.

My Dreams and Aspirations Destroyed

The one thing that halfway saved me from becoming a worse drug addict through high school was boxing. From the time I saw *Rocky*, I knew what I wanted to be when I got older, and I was well on my way. I was going to go to the Olympics and then become the middleweight champion of the world. I had my Lamborghini and house picked out, and that was that. You could not tell me any different. It was a dream I really let nothing interfere with—not girls, not alcohol, not drugs. What I mean is that when I had a fight coming up, I would put it all down and train, make weight, fight, and then I would party.

That all changed in 1982. I was up for the title fight, and had I won this fight I surely would have had a shot at the Olympic trials. Well, I have to tell you that leading up to this fight there was a lot of hoopla. I had won a fight a month before for which I had to lose a lot of weight in two weeks. There was a big write-up in the paper, and I was ready. Sugar Ray was fighting Roberto Duran, not on my card (of course). That was just the era. Fighting was a big thing. And for me it was everything. The stands were packed. I had friends, family, and my girlfriend all there in anticipation.

But the night started off bad. I was overweight hours before the fight, so they gave me a chance to lose it prior to the final weigh-in. It was only maybe half a pound or so, which you can sweat and spit off quickly. And I did. I got in the ring, and the crowd was screaming. The very first round I got my bell rung good. I didn't go down, but I was seeing double for sure. I made it to the middle of the third round (amateur fights are three, two-minute rounds), and they stopped it for a technical knockout! I had never been stopped, and it killed me. Don't get me wrong. This guy was good, and he had me from the first punch. All I could do was try to shove him into the ropes and swing—not my style. Up until then I had won by boxing, moving, and jabbing.

Mr. Summer, the father of one of my best friends, said to me, "Tim, you swung, he countered, and he rocked you every time." I was devastated after that. My life was over as I knew it. This was when my life took a major turn. I picked up a six-pack of tall boys on the way home from that fight and never laced up another pair of gloves competitively.

I was seventeen when my short boxing career ended, and I had one more year of high school left. Most of my close friends were a year older and already off to college. I had other friends, but Joey had gone to school on a golf scholarship, and I was stuck in high school to fend for myself. I was still playing lacrosse, and I was a starting crease attack man that year. My drinking and pot use increased to daily and heavy. I could always play lacrosse, even after an all-night binge.

The day before one of our county's rival games, once again I got into another fight with a guy in school. I was not suspended, but I was not allowed to play in that game. I will never forget my coach saying to me, "I never thought there would come a day when I would be saying this to you, but I was depending on you and need you for this game, and you screwed it up." Man, that felt good and hurt all at the same time. Once again, I saw that look of disappointment. In any case, graduation came. I graduated, somehow, and my high school years were soon behind me.

I reconnected with that lacrosse coach years after high school. When he heard about my work in the community with the sober homes and the recovery movement, he became very interested. On numerous occasions he would call and ask if there was anything we needed for the sober homes and the guys. He pitched in money for them all to go to a Baltimore Orioles game. It took me all of those years when I was finally able to change that look of disappointment in my coach's eyes to a strong look of pride in me.

DWI

After high school, I really had no plans. I couldn't go to any four-year schools because my grades were too bad. So we found a junior college in Texas for me to attend. A junior college is a term that was used a long time ago to describe a two-year school and it often had dorms. I was excited about going there. A friend of mine from school was going with me. It was, in a sense, a new start.

Well, the summer before we left, I had my first encounter with the law. I was driving home from a bar in Catonsville, Maryland. I was drunk, bad drunk as I recall, and I was throwing up out of my truck. I saw lights, red and blue, and that was that. I had a DWI at age seventeen. The thing was that the cop gave me a ride home, and I was off to Texas and school before my dad knew anything. Trust me, that would not happen today. That was in 1983.

I got a slap on the wrist and one year of probation, and I was on my way.

My College Career

Two weeks before school started, my dad, a friend I had graduated high school with, and I were on our way to Texas. It was about a twenty-four-hour drive to Texas from Maryland, and we could not wait to get there. At this time my dad had a farm in Texas. We had land and a cabin. I never figured out why we always called it a farm.

Anyway, we went to the campus first—Henderson County Junior College in Athens, Texas. Then we went to the farm, where my friend and I picked up a quarter pound of weed from an old babysitter of mine and her husband. He was a truck driver and probably one of the craziest people I had met up to this point in my life. We spent a few days at the farm and then went off to school.

So there we were. We had weed, so we were immediately accepted by the partiers, and the party was on. I started classes, and all was going well. I was now free and away from the father I feared. I was able to stay out all night, drink, and get high with no fear of repercussions from my dad. Somehow, I made it through the first semester of school okay. I had a 3.0 grade point average and was actually going to class. The academic side of me has resurfaced now as an addict in recovery, as I am pursuing my degree again.

However, back in those years, my interest in academics was derailed when, one night, we all went to a club in Tyler, Texas. Our school was in a dry county in Texas, so you had to go to another town to go clubbing. I don't remember the name of the club, but I do remember that I was introduced to crystal meth, a drug I had never even heard of prior to this night. I tried it. Why not? Everyone else was doing it, so how bad could it be?

I snorted one line, and I was up (wired to the gills) for fourteen hours at least! I talked, I talked, and did I say I talked, and I mean nonstop. You could not shut me up. I was going up to people I had never met, and by the end of the night I was best friends with everyone in that bar.

So just like finding the answer with that first buzz at the age of thirteen, now I had truly found the answer. It wasn't even three days after that night that I was looking for the guy we got it from. I found him. He invited my roommate and me out to his trailer, and I got it again. This was the point when *everything* was about to change for the worse.

The Needle and The Spoon

There were people at the dealer's trailer who were injecting this drug into their arms with hypodermic needles. Needless to say, I said, "I want to try that." No questions asked, they showed me how.

The drug was drawn up in a spoon, and one of the guys there put a belt around my arm and told me to look away. Then there was a little pinprick, and *boom*, it hit me. Now I had truly found what I had been looking for! It was instant. I was hooked, and I was hooked on the needle. I learned that night that just about anything can be broken down with a little water, drawn into a syringe, and injected. These lessons cannot be learned in school. They are learned along the hard road of life.

From that day forward I never snorted anything ever again. I would have shot up a birth control pill if I thought it might get me high. My addiction was brewing up in me like a hurricane building strength and steam at sea, just looking for a place to land, which would later come to be anyone close to me. My dad, my brothers, Arlene, girlfriends, my children—it did not matter. From this point on it went quickly from a category one storm to eventually a category five at the end! I had a checking account connected to my dad's in Maryland at the time, and I started slowly writing checks for this drug and eventually started not going to class at all. Soon enough there was no more school. I was slowly entering a private hell which kept me captive for much of my adult life.

Fatherhood Begins

It was sometime in the fall of 1984. I was outside my dorm with some friends, and a van drove by. It was a carload of girls. I don't remember all their names, but one of them became the mother of my children. They stopped and told us there was a party that night at one of their houses. They were local girls in the town, not students at the college. Well, one of the girls was obviously interested in me, and I must say I was interested in her. She was a beautiful little Southern girl.

We didn't even really get a chance to go on a date other than that first night at the party, and I was being kicked out of school. The dean of the school had called me into his office. Once again, even in college, I was being called into an office. I was in trouble!

He said, "Mr. Weber, you can't stay on campus anymore. This is not an apartment, and you have no classes. Therefore, I must ask you to leave."

I was devastated but not because I had probably blown my education. No, I might have to move back to Maryland with my dad. This was when I started to become a con and a manipulator. I was able to convince my new girlfriend of two weeks that I was going to have to move back to Maryland if I didn't find a place to stay. I told her I just had dropped a class or two and was below a full-time student load and had to stay somewhere for the semester until next semester. So, she went to her parents, and they agreed to let me stay with them. The truth of the matter was I was out of school completely.

I will admit, I was smitten with the girl. However, the thought of moving back home was out of the question. At the time all this was going down, my father was out of the country on business. So when he returned I was able to fill him in and make him think everything was okay. I would stay with my girlfriend and her family and get back to a full load the next semester.

But that's not what happened. I was using crystal meth as much as possible and getting worse day by day. My girlfriend had no idea. Her family had no idea. The only people who knew were the friend I had come to school with, the guy I got the meth from, and a few other guys at school. Secrets began to rule my life, as drugs became my King.

Megan and Michael

About two weeks after I moved in with my girlfriend, she was pregnant, and Megan was on the way. I was getting so far gone by that point that it was sad. There was no way I was capable of love. I couldn't love anyone, including myself. So, there I was, nineteen, no job, out of school, and let's not forget the hurricane of addiction that was growing daily! We now had to get married (so I thought), and nine months later on September 10, 1985, Megan Ann came into this world.

Now what? I had this beautiful girl I had to take care of. I wanted to, I just didn't know how. I didn't even know what an electric bill was let alone a car payment, insurance, and all the bills that come with being an adult. She was the most beautiful thing I had ever seen. I must say that after seeing, touching, and holding my little girl, I thought, *Okay, it is time for me to quit using drugs. How blessed I am to have a healthy child. It is time for me to grow up.* However, as anyone who has experienced the power of addiction knows, those were just words. The concept of action for change was not in my vocabulary.

Not long after Megan was born, I was back to using as much as possible. I tried to only drink beer, but every time I got drunk, I couldn't control myself, and I was off looking for a shot of meth. Once I did one shot, I would disappear for days. To say the least, it just kept getting worse.

On February 23, 1987, my son, Michael Dale, was born. Again, he was the apple of my eye, a son to carry on the family name. Well, by this point I was most definitely at a category three in my addiction. I was starting to write hot checks and stealing from my wife's parents' flower business, and every word out of my mouth was a lie.

The Flower Business

My father-in-law owned a couple of flower shops at the time, and because I didn't work a steady job, I could always go up there and, deliver, clean and really just steal, if I am being honest. After all, if I was up there working, at least they weren't just giving me money to support my kids, and let's not forget the bad drug habit I had.

I will say this: through my time in the flower shop, I did learn to design flower arrangements, which—as you will see—came in handy through the years and now provides myself and my family a good living. I know my father-in-law knew I was stealing and just didn't have the heart to say anything. He was one of the kindest, most honorable men I have ever known.

It got to the point that every day he had to cash checks to put cash in the drawer to operate. Eventually he just basically gave my wife and me the shop. We started operating it, and I really got to know the flower business. I was trying so hard to be a father, business owner, and husband, but I just could not fight off the demon of addiction. I would do okay for a week or two, and then I was off and running, spending all our money and writing hot checks. I can say that in maybe one year I shot that whole flower shop up my arm! While rose petals are fleeting, and they eventually die after they bloom, so did my self-respect.

The First of Many Rehabs

I must have been about twenty-one years old when I entered my first drug and alcohol rehab. I had no idea what to expect. I just knew this would get everyone off my back. I checked in and started my first shot at recovery. At this point I was someone who needed recovery but by no means wanted it. As you will see later, in order to get recovery, that need most definitely has to turn into a want. I've also learned it's not enough to just want recovery, you have to do the work and take the necessary steps to change.

This is where I was introduced to the 12-Step program that would eventually introduce me to God and save my life. I remember my first meeting was in the cafeteria in the rehab. I sat way in the back, and a group of guys were already up in the front. I think there were three of them. One guy read a bunch of stuff. The other guy just sat there. Then one of them spoke after all the readings, which were quite boring.

The guy who spoke was named Scott. He had a long blond hair and tattoos and looked to be about six feet tall. His face looked very rough, like he'd had a hard life. He stood up and said, "My name is Scott, and I am an alcoholic and drug addict, and thanks to God and the 12-Steps, I did not have to stick a needle in my arm or take a drink of alcohol today."

This caught my attention, so I perked up and listened. I don't remember all that was said that night, but I do remember him saying that because of his addiction he went to prison for fifteen years. Since getting out, he had attended 12-Step meetings on a regular basis and never turned down an opportunity to share his story with others. He said that for him it had taken going to prison, but it did not have to be that way. Anyone could stop now and get into recovery and have a good life.

I felt like he was talking to me. I know now it was most definitely God speaking through this man and planting a seed that would later grow and send me on a mission to help others who have this deadly disease. To see me as a role model for others, back then, it would have been unbelievable.

I wish I could say that was the only rehab I needed, but that is just not the way it was. I would eventually go through around eighteen rehabs, some lasting three days. In a couple of rehabs, I went for a year, another for eighteen months, and in another couple, I went for six months. To go into the story of each one of those rehabs would be impossible, so I will touch on a few throughout this part of the book. I remember getting out of that first rehab and going to my first 12-Step meeting on my own. I was thinking. There is no way I can spend the rest of my life going to these meetings. Everyone in there was over forty and looked very boring. So, I didn't go much more.

Instead I continued to use, and I used whatever I could. Crack had just started getting popular then, and of course I tried it and liked it, so I now had another weapon in my arsenal to feed my addiction. I didn't really like it a lot, but if I couldn't find any meth, I could always find crack, 24-7.

This is the part where everything really got bad. I was doing whatever I had to do to get high. Mostly taking every penny I could from my wife, her family, and even stealing money out of my own kids' piggy banks. Finally, my wife had enough and kicked me out, and I moved to Houston to live with my older brother, Mike, who was going through a divorce at the same time.

My dad had a house there he'd bought as an investment, and Mike had been fixing it up for him. My dad thought it would be a good idea to let me go there and we could lean on each other. Well, we leaned alright. It was two hurricanes of addiction coming together to make the perfect storm. This is where I delved into a drug that would take every ounce of life out of me: heroin. It robbed me of years upon years of freedom and life and almost took my breath (killed me) many times. I thank God for each breath that I take today, in recovery.

Heroin

I was twenty-five years old when I took my first shot of black tar heroin. I was with my brother and some other guys in Houston. We drove to a house in a rough section of the city near the Astrodome. We walked into a house with a mom, a dad, and kids all around. The guy took us to a table in the kitchen, and we all bought a twenty-five-dollar foil of tar.

As my first time with heroin, I had someone break it down for me and draw it into the syringe, and then I took over from there. I had been sticking needles in my arm for years now, so I could do that. I do remember being scared, so I put the needle in and only shot half in. *Bam!* It hit me. *Now that is what I have been looking for!* It gives you a feeling of euphoria that is out of this world. I did not care about anything—no kids, no ex, nothing. I was to the point of comfortably numb. This is where I stayed for the next twelve years. Numb! One of the many bad things about this drug is that it wears off and you get physically-hooked quickly. This is where everything gets foggy, so I will do my best to tell this part as I remember it. These memories are still with me today.

First, I digress for a moment. I have observed that people don't understand that heroin is an opioid drug. Opiates are found in many prescription pain meds. So, I can say that, based on my experience of being hooked, I understand why some people taking pain meds for a prolonged period can get as hooked as I felt on the drugs I took.

I think this reality has been a big factor in the heroin epidemic that is now skyrocketing. Many people start off with prescription pain meds and after they are cut off by the doctor when its time to, people can develop a tendency towards addiction.

Someone with a substance abuse disorder can easily turn to heroin after taking pain meds for a long time. This was not my path to heroin. My path was through recreational drug use. My heart goes out to anybody who needs meds for their pain, and then one day, ends up on heroin.

As I said, there are no pain meds in my story. I started out with doing just heroin, but soon—very soon—started to speedball my stuff. That is when you mix heroin with cocaine and inject it. It is the same concoction that has killed a lot of famous people whose deaths you have heard of. This was where that little boy from the past was buried. I was now a full-blown addict. I had crossed a line where turning back was going to take a miracle, an intervention from God.

My brother and I lived in the house in Houston, supposedly fixing it up. We had bought a shower and tub insert from a store to put into the house. Well, it was about two hundred dollars, so anytime we ran short on money we would return it to get the money and buy heroin. We did this at least three times—bought it, returned it, bought it, returned it, etc. Finally, one time we actually installed it so we couldn't very well return it again. Of course, all this was done on my dad's money. He had an account set up for us so we could buy supplies for the house and for us to live. He was out of the country and had no idea what was going on.

This is where I first developed a very valuable asset I had at this time. I say *asset* in jest. It was the time in my life when I became a master manipulator. I met a girl in Houston who was a single mother, and I went out on a date with her. Why she went, I have no idea, but within the next two days I conned her into letting me move in with her. I took money, food, and anything she had over the small amount of time I spent with her. I even took money out of her account to the point that she couldn't pay her rent.

She came over to our house after I figured I had used her all I could, and tried to wake me up. I was high and not in the mood to listen to this girl gripe at me. I remember her saying, "How could you do this to me and my daughter?" The fact was I did not care. Heck, at this point I didn't care about anyone but myself and feeding my addiction. I was cold as ice—no emotion and no feelings whatsoever.

This went on in Houston a while longer until my dad returned to the United States and we were about to be found out. My brother Pat was living in Maryland at the time, and he was in recovery—a 12-Step program—and doing well. They somehow got wind of what was going on in Texas, and both flew down for an intervention. Within hours I was on a plane on my way to Maryland to go into yet another rehab.

My brother Mike was to stay back and help my dad close the house up. So, I got the better end of that deal and was in rehab with medication to detoxify my heroin addiction, while Mike had to kick his habit in the car with my father all the way from Texas to Maryland, a twenty-four-hour drive straight through.

I got to Maryland and checked into rehab and kicked heroin for the first time. Let me paint a picture for you of coming off a heroin addiction. It feels like the worse flu you have ever imagined. Your bones ache to the core, your nose runs nonstop, you have uncontrollable diarrhea, and your stomach aches with cramps. You are cold and chilled one minute and hot the next, and the depression makes you want to die! And this was in rehab, so I know my brother was really going through it worse. The one thing about heroin withdrawal is that it won't kill; you just want to kill yourself. If you do heroin for three days in a row, you are going to go through some kind of withdrawal.

Well, I got out of rehab and was now living in Maryland. An old high school friend came to see me at the rehab and offered me a job when I got out. I hadn't been to Maryland in years, so it was nice to have a change, and I felt good and healthy after rehab. My brothers were both there, and we saw each other a lot and even went to meetings together. So, there I was living back in Maryland and working for my friend, and all was well. But recovery did not come first, and God was nowhere in the picture, so it wasn't long before I thought, *Well, maybe I can just drink beer.* Wrong!

It's important to say at this point in my story that I've learned, in the recovery process that you can't just up and quit using drugs cold turkey. That is very rare. You need a complete spiritual awakening. It took me a long time to realize this. It's so hard for young people to stop thinking that drinking and smoking weed are not an issue, not something to sweat over. I certainly couldn't stop oversimplifying it.

In reality, if you are a person who suffers from a substance use disorder, you might become addicted to anything that alters your mind and offers you tremendous pleasure. I was no different.

I often use this example. If you've already done heroin, let's equate the experience with going skiing or snowboarding. Yes, these are positive experiences. But the way in which they advance helps shed some light on the addiction process. The beginner trails in these sports are like the start of using drugs or alcohol—slow and steady, at times. If you've already gone down the steeper trails, you will always be seeking a "higher high." When it comes to drugs, the harder the better.

Back to my new stint in Maryland. I was working for my friend at the deli and decided to start making some extra money by selling candy arrangements. It was an idea I picked up working for a company in Houston during the beginning stages of my heroin addiction. I worked for the company for maybe two weeks. At the time I was already hooked on heroin and ended up stealing all the money out of the register and never going back.

Having floral experience from my work at my ex-father-in-law's shop, it was very easy to pick this craft up. A candy arrangement was a bouquet made out of candy. They were really cool-looking. So, I started making them around Christmastime and selling them at the deli, and it was not long before I was getting many orders. So, being the entrepreneur that I was, I was ready to quit the deli and go out on my own. I have really always had that entrepreneurial spirit in me. It's just that the spirit of addiction always won. I talked to my friend, and he was behind me. In fact, he wanted in on it, and he put up the money to get us started. We found a spot in the mall in Columbia, Maryland (actually a kiosk) and were soon in business.

It all started off good, and we were selling bouquets and having fun. I had my friend Joey as sales manager, and he was getting hospital accounts, and we were on our way. Just one big problem was about to interfere: me and my addiction. I had started drinking, and Joey and I were having fun almost like we were in high school again. One night we were out at a bar, and I got drunk and left, and went into Baltimore and found some heroin.

Just like I have said with the skiing analogy, the beginner trail that I compare to the start of "using" can be a quick spiral into the black diamond. The black diamond is the high peak of an advanced-level ski trail. When it comes to alcohol and drugs, a fall from this peak of artificial intoxication can land you quickly into rehab. This analogy should be understandable to sports enthusiasts and non-sporting folks alike, because anyone can fall into the abyss of addiction. That's my personal observation—sad, but true.

Here's another observation: if you're an addict and an alcoholic, you cannot try to substitute one for the other. That means if you are a crack addict and you drink again, you are going to go back to using crack.

And if you are a heroin addict, you are going to use heroin again. I put this to the test for many years, and whether it was the first night I drank or two months later, I always went back to heroin—always.

So that night I went to the worst part of Baltimore I could find, drove by a corner, saw what I thought—no, what I knew—were dealers and asked if they knew where I could get some boy. Boy is a street name for heroin in Texas, but obviously it was not called that here. They looked at me like I was crazy, so I rephrased it and found out that in Baltimore it was called dope. And they even gave the dope a name like Suicide, Bin Laden, Killa, etc.

Well, needless to say, I picked up the lingo quickly. One name that was the same everywhere was girl. That was cocaine. So, I got a couple of pills of dope and two caps of girl, and I was off and running again. I was able to hide this part of my addiction for a little while and just let a few people know I was drinking. The friend who was my partner in the candy business was very upset, and he had good reason. I was about to lose all the money he had invested.

Kentucky

It was not long after we opened our business that I ran into an old girlfriend who was visiting Maryland from her hometown in Kentucky. She had moved from Maryland to Kentucky years before. We had originally met at our Maryland high school. Her name is Mary and we started seeing one another again. The thing was she knew me very well, and she had heard about my stints in rehab and was well aware of the fact that I was an alcoholic and an addict.

So, while Mary was in town for a while with her daughter Polly, Mary and I started a fast and furious relationship. We had dated in high school, and to my surprise I discovered that she had been in love with me since. So, there it was, almost ten years after high school, and we both were parents and back together. After spending those few days together, we really wanted it to go further. All the time I was hiding the fact that I was drinking and drugging again.

After about a week or two of her going back home to Kentucky, she asked me to come see her, or I asked her if I could come see her. I am not really sure who asked whom. In any case, I went to see her, and that visit changed her and Polly's life for a long time. I went back to Maryland after a few days, and we talked on the phone every day. I was now most definitely at a category four of my addiction and about to hit Kentucky, and to strike at the lives of Mary and Polly. No foul-weather storm could have impacted them harder than my personal hurricane did.

I had an old car—I think it was a '78 Ford Fairmont—so we talked about trying to have a long-distance relationship. The problem was that my old car barely got me to and from the mall, so there was no way it would go back and forth to Kentucky. She had an extra car she didn't use—a Porsche to boot. She said I could fly up and drive home to Maryland so I could work the business and then drive to see her as often as I could. We went for a little while with me driving back and forth from Maryland to Kentucky. I was drinking again pretty heavily and driving to Baltimore and doing heroin—all in Mary's car.

Well, things started really heating up between us, and things were not going too good at the business because I was back on drugs. Not only was I spending all the money, but I wasn't even showing up at work. So, one day, I was on the phone with Mary, crying the blues and missing her and her missing me.

"Just move here," she said.

"Okay," I said.

The next day I went to the mall before it opened and cleared out my cart. I think I even threw a lot of stuff in the dumpster. I then headed for Kentucky. This caused one of my best friends and I to go our separate ways in anger. He was angry and rightly so. It was all his money going down the drain.

I know now that he always knew I was a messed-up addict and about to ruin Mary's life. He was right. I tried for many years to repair this relationship with him. The fact is I always tried when I wasn't serious about recovery. I hope one day to make amends with him. We probably won't ever be as good friends as we were years ago, but I would still like to look him in the eye and apologize, for him to know I mean it.

If Mary only knew about the nightmare that I was about to put her and Polly through. I moved in, and I just kept getting worse. Mary owned a horse farm in Kentucky and was raising racehorses. I must be honest. It was quite overwhelming. The place was unbelievable. Here I was trying once again to stay clean and start a new life. The one thing about the disease of addiction is that if not treated, it just lays dormant, waiting for the right opportunity to rear its ugly head.

I was just trying with all of my heart not to use. Over and over again—I tried so hard! If there's one thing I've learned in recovery, it's that just changing my geographical location in hopes of getting rid of familiarity and stopping drug use is no way to treat the disease itself. I tried this method of fleeing my habit for new scenery and a new life so many times. I failed every time, until I sincerely embraced all aspects of recovery and the daily work that it takes to succeed.

Anyway, back to my story about moving in with Mary. Things were great at first, but they went bad quickly. I was living with a girlfriend who was a successful businesswoman in her field, and the best I could do was make seven dollars an hour at a plant in Lexington, Kentucky. I just did not feel good about myself, and what I did when I felt bad was to use drugs. For that moment, I didn't feel better, but at least I was high and didn't feel. This was much better than the emotions I carried inside.

It was not long before I started taking money from her credit cards and any loose money she left around the house. Around Easter that year some of her family came in for the holiday. I left that Friday to supposedly look for a job. I was really out smoking crack. I had even driven up to the farm late one night that weekend and snuck into the barn where she kept the horse tranquilizers. I rifled through the small refrigerator and found some ACE, an animal tranquilizer I had watched her for months shoot into the veins of the necks of big racehorses. They were tranquilized to get them on a trailer.

I had been smoking crack only because I couldn't find heroin, so I needed something to slow me down, and I thought if this stuff knocked a horse out, maybe a small amount would make me feel just right. I even remember her asking me time and time again, "Does this bother you?" when she was injecting a horse. I would always reply, "No. I am done with that life." As you will see, I was not to be done for many years.

I got the ACE out of the fridge, found a horse needle that probably had a point on it the size of a matchstick, drew up a small amount, dropped my pants, and jabbed the needle in my rear end. I was too scared to stick it in my vein, so a muscle shot would have to do. I put it all up, walked out of the barn, and collapsed. I looked up at the stars and wondered if I had made a mistake. The fact is that years later when Mary found out I had done this, she told me that if I had picked the other tranquilizer—I am not sure of the name—it would have killed me on the spot!

Surely, God was looking over me at that moment! There was a bigger plan in store for me to help others down the road in my life and it just wasn't my time to go yet, when I gave myself the injection that I actually lived through.

As it turned out, I woke up before dawn and drove off to spend another day smoking crack. I often wondered how I drove up to the barn with the whole family there and no one knew. I stayed away until late Sunday night so that I would show up after they had already left. Or so I thought. Her mom was still there, and when I walked in, I was surprised to say the least. Mary looked at me with the most disappointed, ashamed, and embarrassed look. It was a look I was starting to grow accustomed to.

She said, "You are going to have to leave."

I knew that was coming and was prepared for it. But I was not expecting to be on an airplane back to Maryland with her mom. Mary told me before I left that if I asked her mom, she would get me into

Father Martin's Ashley, a rehab in Maryland. Her family was a big contributor to Father Martin's.

I waited until I got on the ground in Baltimore before I popped the question. We didn't sit together on the plane, and honestly, I was glad because I was extremely ashamed.

I walked up to her and asked, "Would you please help me get into rehab?"

She looked at me and said, "You come out to my house tomorrow, and I will talk to you about it."

I drove out the next day, and I was in rehab within a few days after talking with Mary's mom.

I actually completed the full 30 days with a couple of visits from Mary. The plan was for me to graduate and leave the treatment center and go to a halfway house for six months. Soon after moving into the halfway house, I started to use again. Like with previous programs, I didn't follow through with what I was supposed to do, like getting a sponsor and making recovery a priority. I was kicked out of the halfway house for using. Eventually, I decided to leave Maryland and move back to Texas.

Texas Tornado

I had now burned my bridges in Maryland and Kentucky. So, I thought I would go back to Texas and move to Dallas. I would be closer to my kids and could start over. I had been away long enough that it felt like a new place. My dad once again, being the enabler-father that he was, hooked me up with a car and an apartment in "Big D" (Dallas). I called my kids, Megan and Michael. They were probably nine and eleven years old by then. I had seen them off and on through the last couple of years and talked to them as often as I could when I was not getting high somewhere. My dad had always paid for them to come up to Maryland to see me.

I had a nice apartment and was back on track for a month or so. I got a job in the floral department of a big superstore chain. Once again, my floral background came in handy. I was hired on the spot and met many new friends. I was doing okay. I kept being an addict and an alcoholic a secret, and I would go out drinking with people from work. After all, I was in a new place and thought that maybe I could handle it this time. But like I said before, if you are an alcoholic, you are an addict, too. I have found that you will always go back to your drug of choice. Some people may not agree with this, but they just haven't experienced it yet. There is a difference between someone who just drinks too much and an alcoholic—it is the phenomenon of craving, the obsession that once started, can't be stopped without an interruption. For me, the interruption came in the form of rehabs.

The Original Candy Arrangement

had been working at the store for maybe two months and actually thinking, *Maybe I have this drinking under control. I am working and going out and having a few beers like all my normal friends. So no drugs—yet!* I talked the people I worked for into letting me sell some of my candy arrangements through the store, and while they did not do well there, they did get noticed.

A manager from a large grocery store chain saw them and called me and said, "You have to take samples of these to my corporate office. I love them and want them in my store."

I called the corporate office, and the receptionist said, "You have to send a brochure, and we will contact you if we think we can sell it."

In other words, she was blowing me off.

I said, "Miss, I don't have a brochure. Can I come by and drop off a couple of samples?"

"Sure," she said, and she gave me the address.

The next day I was there and dropped off a couple, and the rest is history. They loved them, I got a call, and they wanted to set up an appointment to meet my partner and me.

My business partner was once again a victim of my disease. Her name was Julie, and she worked at the same place I did. We made eye contact one day, and that was that. I found out she was married, so I thought, *Well, I might as well forget this girl.* I was wrong. She was very persistent and wanted to go out one night. I knew it was wrong, but at this point I was not Mr. Moral. In fact, everything I did was wrong and immoral. We started a serious affair, and it was intense to say the least.

I talked her into getting into this business with me for one reason— no two: she had money, and we were dating. So we met with the buyer for the floral department of this big chain store, and we were in. They tested us in five stores, and within two weeks they approved us for all sixty stores throughout Dallas-Fort Worth. Man, what a trip! Look what I had done. This was amazing. Look at me, look at me! That's the way I was, very arrogant and cocky on the outside and the most insecure, self-centered, jealous man on the planet on the inside.

We were on our way and making some money for a little while. Julie had to put everything in her name and put up all the money. She put all her trust in me; she even quit her job to work there with me. We rented a warehouse in Irving, Texas, right next to the Cowboy's stadium. We were pumping out bouquets, and we started to get in over our heads.

I called my brother Mike, who was back in Houston at this time, and asked him if he wanted a job. He did not hesitate. He and his two little girls moved up to the Dallas area. Mike was clean at the time and taking care of his girls on his own, and I am sure he thought I was clean too. The fact is that I was not using drugs, just drinking.

But it was not long after Mike got up there that I ran into a guy at his apartment and had a beer with him. The subject of heroin came up, and he knew right where to get it. So once again I was off and running, and in a matter of a few months I racked up ten thousand dollars in hot checks and was hooked on heroin, and I mean hooked bad. I was using every day and a lot of it.

This was around the time the famous white Bronco chase was going on, and I remember watching the start of the trial and thinking I was worse off than him. Julie and Mike had left, and I was living in the shop, taking showers in the sink. I was a mess and strung out worse than ever. The electricity was about to get shut off, I had no car, I was stuck in that shop with nowhere to go, and I surely couldn't write any more checks that were hot. I would have; it's just that no one would take them.

The events I just described were a perfect example of why someone who suffers with a substance use disorder can be dually-addicted. If you drink alcohol and are a drug addict, you will go back to that drug or you will go back to alcohol. The point is I could not limit myself to one or the other. I started embracing both alcohol and drugs and my world was turning worse than ever before.

Suicide Attempt

I was watching the trial of the century on TV and feeling very sick from withdrawal. I decided I couldn't take it anymore. I pulled out a razor blade and started slicing my left wrist. I was cutting so deeply that my pinky and ring finger twitched with every cut. I hit a vein that started shooting blood out in a stream. I thought, *Okay, I did it.* I lay there bleeding and fell asleep. To my surprise, I woke up with the sun beaming through the front windows of the shop, and it was the worse feeling in the world. I got up, wrapped an old dirty sock around my wrist, and called my drug buddy to come pick me up so I could try to cash a check. We were persistent. I tried enough places and finally got one cashed for three hundred dollars.

It was sometime during my "Texas Tornado" summer, when it is always hot, that I was wearing a sweat jacket to hide my needle marks. I was also hiding the sock filled with blood I had wrapped around my arm. I checked into a motel and sent my buddy to score me some heroin and cocaine, mostly coke. I had planned that night to do one big shot and explode my heart and die. So he left and headed for Oak Cliff to score, and I waited for what seemed like hours. When he returned, he had a case of beer and some pot. He said, "Sorry, dude. I couldn't find any boy or girl," which meant heroin and cocaine.

That was a lie. I had never gone looking for dope and couldn't find it. So, he left, and I was there all alone with beer and weed—not my cup of tea at all. I surely smoked it and drank it anyway.

At this time my brother had gone by the candy shop to check on me, walked in, and saw a puddle of blood the size of a good-sized kitchen table. He was scared to death and thought someone had killed me and dumped me in a dumpster somewhere.

Sometime that night I called him from the hotel and he told me if I called Jim—a guy we had met at a meeting—he knew a place in Mabank, Texas, where I could go for treatment. I thought, *there is no way I am going to treatment*. But after sitting in that motel room, with check-out time approaching, no car, no money, and of course no dope, I was up against a brick wall. I had no choice, so I called him.

This was without question one of the darkest times of existence. Fortunately, a new door will open in the next chapter of my life, as I am about to meet someone who will change me forever. Stay tuned. My story eventually gets better from here, but not without some more serious ups and downs.

The House of Isaiah

This is most definitely where the seed of God was sown into my heart. It was a long-term rehab way out in the country, miles from any paved road let alone a highway. I walked into the office, and this big man was sitting behind a desk. He peered at me over his glasses. "Son, you ready to give God a try?" he asked. His name was Isiah. He ran the House of Isaiah (which is spelled differently than his actual name).

I replied, "Sure. I am dying out there."

"Well, if you give six months of your life, I will help you," he said with a serious look.

I thought, *Well, I have nowhere else to go.* I didn't say that, just thought it.

This is where I first heard, "If you want something you have never had, you must be willing to do something you have never done." Isiah said it all the time. I now always include that quote, which I heard so many years ago, whenever I tell my story.

I spent about two months there, left against the wishes of Isiah, and returned to my old life. I started using right away, and this is when I started my life of crime and homelessness. Remember, I said earlier that things were going to turn around for me. They will, just after the rollercoaster ride ends.

You Have the Right
to Remain Silent

I was out of the House of Isaiah for a few months, not going to meetings, not praying, not doing anything to try to stay clean. I got back together with my kids' mom sometime after I got out of the House of Isaiah for the first time. I was working in Dallas for a flower shop and stopped by a sports bar on the way home and drank a beer, and then another and another. Well, that was that. I went to Oak Cliff to find Randy, the guy I used to do heroin with when I had the candy business. It didn't take long. I found him, and I was back on heroin and hooked within days.

I hid it from my work, kids, and ex-wife for a while, but it was all about to be revealed. Randy and I were driving very late one night in a bad part of Dallas. We had just scored about eight baskets. A basket is one pill of heroin and one pill of cocaine, and a pill is a gelcap filled with the drug. We were on our way out of the neighborhood, and there they were: red and blue lights. It was 3:00 a.m., and I was in a neighborhood you don't drive through at that time, actually at any time. It was a drug-infested area, and you were only there for one reason: drugs. We saw the lights, and I said, "Eat it!" We both had four baskets. I ate mine, and I thought he ate his too.

"Sir, could you step out of the car? What brings you to this side of town?" the officer asked. Make no mistake, he knew.

"We were trying to score but couldn't find any," I replied.

"Let me see your arms," he demanded. I had fresh tracks and many old tracks. Tracks are the point of entry where the needle goes in. "Well, you have done a shot recently. I see blood on your arm and sleeve."

"I've got one," the officer's partner said from the driver's side of the car.

I wondered how in the world they had found something we ate. His partner brought back one basket he had found on the driver's side floorboard and laid it on the trunk.

"Sir, you have the right to remain silent..." You get the point.

I was booked into Dallas County Jail on April Fool's Day of 1996 for possession of a controlled substance. I really tried to stay clean from that point on and just couldn't. I went to court a few months later and got a two-year suspended sentence and five years' probation. Let me tell you, this is how powerful addiction can be. I knew if I failed a urinalysis, I was going to jail for two years. That was not enough to stop me from going out drinking and eventually losing my job, getting kicked out of my ex-wife's house again, and not seeing my kids. I was hooked again and now on probation.

Drug Motels

I was in Dallas and started staying in drug motels throughout the city. There are many motels around the area that are plagued with drugs and prostitution. I mean 24-7 drugs, and girls are out there even as I write this book. I lived in these places off and on for years. I would go out and steal beer from a grocery store, usually ten or so cases, and take them around and sell them at construction sites, corners, or even the motel I was staying at. I would get ten dollars per case, keep one to drink, and then pay for my hotel room and get my drugs.

This went on every day for months. I didn't really consider this my homeless state. After all, I was in a place with a bed, a shower, and a roof. I was sinking further and further into the world of crime that went along with being a street junkie. As long as I was able to get high, everything was okay. It is so sad to look back on that life today and remember those feelings. It was sick, and I didn't even feel like I was that bad off. Sitting where I am today, in the comfort of the home which we own, it is surreal to me now that I had gone so far downhill.

There is a whole other world out there that many people don't even know exists. That world! These are people just like me—addicts and alcoholics who don't even realize there is a better way of life. I hope and pray that this book will be passed on to someone so that he or she can someday see what I see today. There are literally hundreds of junkies in and out of these hotels at any given time—some old, some kids, some moms, dads, and even grandparents. They are there, and if they are weekend warriors, they don't realize how close they are to being sucked into the life full time.

I remember one time I had stolen some cartons of cigarettes and was trying to sell them with some dude I met in one of these seedy motels. He got out of my car, which by the way was stolen, and he took the cigarettes I had stolen! Well, that was not going to fly. I went looking for him around the different motels and found him. He was in a room, and I was standing outside my car, screaming, "Get your butt out here, you freaking punk!"

He did, and let's just say he wasn't too scared. He came toward me, and I had a crowbar behind my back. I brought it around and took a swing. I missed! He looked at me, grinned, and said, "You just dug your grave, cracker!"

He lunged at me, and we fell back into the car.

I thought I was dead. Somehow, I held on to that crowbar and was able to get it upside his head. He backed up, blood pouring out of his head. He started stumbling over toward a pickup truck, I'm sure to find something to get out and start hitting me with, or a gun. I am not too sure which.

He had dropped three cartons of my cigarettes on the pavement when he came at me. Needless to say, I got them and was very proud of myself, and gained some serious street cred. Even though I spent significant time in the boxing ring, it was no assurance that I could defend myself—especially since I was strung out on drugs and my consciousness was altered. Don't forget, I had not eaten or slept for quite some time. The bad thing was I found out later that night that this guy had just gotten out of prison after doing fifteen flat (that is fifteen straight years).

I did not get much rest that night back in my room. I slept with my crowbar and jumped at every sound I heard. The next night me and another guy were driving around in that stolen car. I never knew from who or where the car had been stolen. I just knew I was driving a hot car. We had stolen some beer earlier that afternoon, so I had money and was looking for some dope and then a room. As it turned out, we didn't get any heroin, but we got some crack and were pulling into a motel to get a room. Once again I saw red and blue lights.

This time I had too much to eat, so I tried to hide it. They shined a light on the car and had us step out and walk backward to the sound of their voice, yes just like on the *Cops* show. And that was that. I was arrested for possession of cocaine and unauthorized use of a motor vehicle. I was in big trouble, and believe it or not, I was relieved. It was like, okay, well, it is over. Now I will have to quit. It will be in prison, but I will be clean and come out clean.

That is a crazy thought, but I do remember those thoughts going through my head. Plus, the guy I smashed with the crowbar was looking for me, and I had heard when any of them saw the car, they were going to start shooting! So going into jail didn't seem all that bad.

At the time, it seemed like jail was the perfect place to be. I often share this perspective with parents and family of addicts who want their loved ones to avoid incarceration.

I was booked into the Dallas County jail almost one year after the last arrest, only this was a worse charge, and I was on probation. After about a week in there, I called my dad and told him what was going on and that I was probably not going to get out of this one. He flew from Maryland to come see me, and the look on his face was the same look I had seen for years from anyone who loved me: shame and disgust, but also some fear. He was scared I was going to prison. The sad thing was that at this point in my addiction, people were happier when I was in jail. At least then they knew I was alive. It is a look I hope I never have to see again from anyone for the rest of my life.

In sharp contrast, today I notice expressions of pride on the faces of family and friends. The happiness I feel because of those expressions of love now brings tears of joy to my eyes.

After sitting in jail for about a week one day, a correctional officer escorted me to a separate room outside of my cell. This was the second jail time for me, so I had no idea what was about to happen and the experience was in some ways still new to me.

As I walked into the room there were two guys in ski masks with badges hanging from around their necks. There was also one detective present. They asked me, "Son, you realize you're in a lot of trouble?"

I searched my brain for an answer and blurted, "The cocaine was not mine!"

They said, "Well, you're already on probation for possession of heroin. You are about to be charged with a stolen vehicle and possession of cocaine." That could have put me in prison for a really long time.

At that point, I was very rattled, so I asked for a cigarette. Apparently, I asked the wrong officer. He sarcastically snapped and said, "Screw you, this isn't a TV show where you get to make one request of us."

The detective with no ski mask on agreed to give me a cigarette, which quickly calmed me down.

They proceeded to tell me that if I turned in three people, they would drop my charges. I was puffing nervously away on my cigarette, and the wheels of my brain were grinding. I realized they are throwing me a law enforcement deal—"three will set you free." By that they mean, take six months to turn in three people and if you don't, you get picked up again by the cops. The appeal of the deal is that if I turned in three people, I could be released and go home that very day.

It wasn't a hard decision because at the time, I didn't want to be a "rat" or a "narc" by snitching to save my own tail.

Also, I had two small children to think about. I was concerned for my family and I told them so. Retaliation was a great fear of mine. Respectfully, or from their point of view disrespectfully, I declined the offer.

They were pissed and I could tell. Suddenly, it was time to go back to my cell. Of course, they took the half-smoked cigarette back from me.

Snitching is a word with lots of baggage for people in recovery. Snitching has a terrible connotation because people tend to think of it as similar to what law enforcement asked of me, which was to "rat" on someone.

The term snitching—in recovery—can be confused with having a friend who is using, going to a probation officer or a family member, or confronting the friend directly. People may feel like they are snitching, when in fact they are saving a life. I am making an important distinction here. Getting help for someone who needs it takes bravery, courage, and good intentions. It is not throwing the person under the bus or some kind of betrayal.

Going back to that jail time I did: A miracle happened after I sat in jail for about three weeks. I was called out of my cell, taken to a room, and told I was being released. The court-appointed attorney told me the car had been taken from someone who had rented it from a car rental place, and they did not want to press charges. That meant that with no stolen car charge, the cocaine couldn't be pinned on me. I didn't really understand that, but I didn't care. I was free and walked out of jail—finally.

The House of Isaiah (Round Two)

This was a big turning point for me. It was the first time I made a smart decision. You see, I had a choice to go back to the motels or call Isiah. I chose Isiah and called him. Luckily, he let me back in. I made the right decision. Then, I stayed there for more than a year this time and was on my way to a glorious Christian walk.

When I got back to the House of Isaiah, I was in trouble with probation. I had Isiah call the probation office, and it was all worked out. All I had to do was complete the program, and I would be out in good standing with probation.

Well, that turned out to be a tough task. Isiah was very hard on me this time around. I remember one time I had been there for around three months and was about to go on a pass to see my kids. Literally, the day they were to pick me up to go see them, he called me into his office and said, "Son, I am not going to let you go on this pass."

I remember thinking, *"How can you do this? My kids are on their way.* I just said, "Okay, Isiah. Amen," and went back to my room and probably flipped out. But I knew to not let Isiah see this because a lot of times it was a test to see how you would react. He told me later that he wanted me to see what it would be like to be in prison and not see my kids at all. He was always doing things that seemed crazy. For example, he sometimes woke us up at two in the morning to have a complete room and dorm change. This was a lesson in dealing with unmet expectations.

Another time, he had me in charge of a group of guys planting bushes in front of the main house. Well, I had been up most of the night with a newcomer to the house. So after planting the bushes, I lay down for a nap. All of the sudden, I heard this screaming from the yard.

"Tim Weber, get out here! You call this a good job? Look at the line of bushes. One of them is out of place!" he screamed, in that kind of voice he used when he was not happy.

I kid you not, there was one bush an inch off from the rest of them. "Dig them all up and replant 'em," he said.

"Are you freaking kidding me? What is your problem with me Isiah?" I screamed. "I am not doing it. I will leave before I dig those up," I said, knowing for sure that I would go straight to jail if I left rehab.

Needless to say, I calmed down and was out digging until late that night. At the time I really thought Isiah hated me, but I grew to understand that he loved me and all of us at the House of Isaiah. He was really teaching us so much about acceptance, patience, and how to deal with unmet expectations. Isiah was an ex-pro football player and dynamic speaker. I won't tell his story, but he had been there, and God called him to save the sick. By that I mean, people just like me. These people are young men with addictions, just like me.

In my opinion, there is no other place around like the House of Isaiah. I will be forever indebted to him for the God he introduced to me, my Lord and Savior Jesus Christ.

It's important to note that Isiah's action have had an incredible ripple effect with people who I help today. I hold them accountable like Isiah did with me. In operating my sober homes, I would sometimes move people from one house to the other or change house managers to show residents that life is full of changes and we all need to deal with the unexpected. This was lesson number one, which Isiah gave me. In a true ripple effect manner, I passed along the lesson to the people I help today. My wish is that they can one day find the hope that I did, and the passion for helping others that I treasure so much.

When my time was up at the House of Isaiah, I was sent to another place for another six months. It was sort of a halfway house with very strict rules and was another place where the Word of God and a 12-Step program were the focus. I really did well there. I completed the program and moved out into a little apartment in Dallas, got a job at a flower shop in the area, and thought I had made it. I was going to a few 12-Step meetings a week but not getting involved in the program. I had no sponsor, I wasn't working the steps, and I had stopped going to church and even praying. All I did was work, stop by a meeting late, leave early, come home, and maybe see my kids on the weekends.

It was not long before I picked up a drink, and soon after I started smoking crack. At first—like always—I hid it from work, girlfriends, and my kids. But the disease of addiction is very progressive, even when we are not using. It sounds strange, but it is most definitely true. Within a month, I had lost my job and was back on heroin and in that same boat. About a week after losing my job, my car was repossessed, and my phone was ringing off the wall. I was back in debt, strung out, had no car, and was disappointing my kids once again. I can't explain how bad it feels when you know you have just screwed everything and everyone around you yet again.

During this time period, I and a friend were robbing stores for money and using my car to get away. The guy I was with felt guilty and wanted to turn himself in. I was scared too. My last hope was to call my Dad again. This short period of time was the worse for me, because my life turned into a crime spree. I was not safe from the law and from local drug dealers. My friend ultimately turned himself in. But I chose to run from Texas.

At this point, I had no choice but to call my dad and beg for a plane ticket to come back to Maryland. Dad did not know any of what I was doing. But, like always, he got me a ticket, and I was on a plane that day.

The Dating Service

Within one day of being back in Columbia, Maryland (the town near Baltimore, but more suburban, and where I grew up), I got a job with my brother Pat. The job was with a dating service where he was working. I was a telemarketer, and we called people who requested a call for information about our service. It was a really easy job, and I worked for my brother, who was the boss of the center. So once again, I had it easy. I had a car given to me by my father and was making some money, and all was well in Tim's world, for a minute. My friend, Joey, was in Maryland, and we hooked up again and were both actually going to meetings together and trying to stay sober.

Well, my former girlfriend, Mary, and I met up again and I was back in her and Polly's lives. Mary had sold her farm in Kentucky and had bought a beautiful farm in Maryland to be closer to her family. It wasn't long before I was living with Mary again at her farm in Maryland. I was working at the dating service and living with Mary, and I started using again. Not much as first, just a few Vicodin with a girl I worked with.

Anyone who knows the disease of addiction would have known I was about to head right back to heroin. And I did very soon. I had gotten a promotion at the dating service and was now a sales rep, which meant I met with people and tried to sell them a service. The services cost anywhere from one thousand dollars to three thousand dollars. I was always shocked when I made a sale. After all, these people were paying all this money for a chance to meet their soul mates. It really did work for some of them, and they would even send in letters letting us know that they were getting married.

Code Blue Overdose

I was working for the same dating service, after my promotion to a sales position from the telemarketing position. I commuted to Fairfax, Virginia. Believe it or not, I was using.

I was shooting heroin and cocaine (speedballs). I had done one before I got to work, and after I was there, I hid a syringe in the office. I was with a client and had just made a big sale, so I grabbed my syringe and went to the bathroom. I pulled the syringe out of my sock and sat on the toilet. I stuck the needle in my arm, shot the dope, stuck the syringe back in my sock, walked out, and went to the gift shop in the office building. My office was in a big office building along with a lot of other businesses. As I walked into the gift shop, I remember putting some Starbursts on the counter, and then I started shaking, and that is all I remember until waking up in an ambulance.

"Tim, Tim, can you hear me?" the paramedic was asking me. "We know your history," he said, meaning they knew I was a heroin addict. One of the girls at the office had told them.

They had shot me full of NARCAN®, a drug to reverse the effects of heroin. I was taken to the hospital and released a few hours later. Mary had come to pick me up, and we went home to her house. I had another pill of heroin and the syringe still on me and pulled it out at home and told Mary, "That's it, I am done." I flushed it down the toilet and thought, *I almost died. I will never do this again.*

It amazes me to this day how they didn't find that syringe and pill of dope. I found out the next day that I had been blue, foaming at the mouth, and not breathing. I had been dead in the courtyard! My friend at work called me and told me all this the next day. I remember her saying, "Dude, did you see God: Because you were dead, Tim."

Well, I didn't see God, but I really thought that this was going to be it. I really wanted to quit doing heroin and get straight, but the very next day when that heroin withdrawal kicked in later that morning, I was on my way to Baltimore. I went to one of my street corners, found two pills of heroin and two pills of coke, went to an abandoned house with some other addicts, and got high for the next three days. At the time, I was stealing disposable cameras from different superstores and selling them at bars in Baltimore and then using the money to get high. I would do this all day. Then at some point during the night, I would lay down on some old newspapers and try to sleep until that insistent urge from the heroin would wake me up and I was off to do it another day.

One thing I've learned through my own experience and that of others is that the first overdose is scary, but overdoses after that are just a part of the drug game. This is when I started my long stretches of homelessness. Mary finally had enough, and we went our separate ways. I don't blame her at all for that. I know all she ever wanted was for me to be clean and sober, either with her or without her.

The Bottom Starts Now

I was living in an abandoned row house on Washington Boulevard in Baltimore, Maryland. This is where I lived on and off for the last year of my addiction, and let me tell you, it was hell on earth. The place had no electricity, no running water, and no toilet. It was nasty. There would be people in the house at all times, some upstairs shooting dope and some at the kitchen table smoking crack. Prostitutes would do their thing in different rooms, usually getting just enough money to do a shot of dope, and then they would hit the street to find another "John" to get money from. We ripped people off who would come to the city, looking for dope. I had become a street rat, just looking for any way I could get ten dollars. I did a lot of "boosting"—that is stealing stuff from stores and then either returning it to the same store I stole it from, or selling it to someone at a hole-in-the-wall bar in the city. I did this every day.

At one point, I ran into a guy who had some fake money—kind of monopoly-type money, only better, and late at night you could rip off dope dealers on the streets. I had stolen a lot of this money from the guy who had it, so I was on a run for a while with this scam. I got really stupid, and I even started doing it during the day. This was very dangerous, and I had bricks thrown through my car window, knives thrown at me, and guns drawn on me many times for this craziness. Yet, I would stay in the same ten-mile radius because that was where

I knew my dope was, and that was where I laid my head every day. I woke up every day and wanted to die. Every day! It was hell, but I just did not know how to stop.

I was getting further and further into this street lifestyle. It is sad, but the people I ran the streets with were just like me. They were lost and just needed to open their hearts, let God in, and try recovery. They are there right now, hoping someone will save them, but just not knowing who that is, wishing they could change, wishing they could live life and not just exist. I know it as sure as I am sitting here writing this story.

I can't explain the emptiness you feel when you pull yourself up off a floor in an abandoned house and walk the streets, looking for a cigarette butt to try to get at least two hits off of and then figuring out how to get ten dollars to get your first shot of the day, all the while the Ravens are playing, the sun is shining, and people are walking to the stadium. They are smiling, laughing, wearing their jerseys, and living life. It feels like crap. So you find your ten dollars, do your shot, and hope it is of good quality so you can attempt to hide these emotions and move forward through the rest of that day.

I overdosed two more times during this period. Once I was driving my car, pulled over, and did a shot of heroin. I stuck the needle in the trunk, pulled out of the gas station, got to a light under the I-95 bridge and Washington Boulevard, and just blacked out. I stopped breathing. I woke up to paramedics, the police and a fire truck. They were shaking me and asked me what I had taken. They had shot me full of NARCAN®, so they knew it was heroin or some kind of opiate. I refused treatment, and I kid you not, they let me just pull my car over to the side and wait a while until I could leave.

This was one of the times I somehow had a car, so one of the ways I would get money was by "hacking." Hacking is picking up people in the city who needed a ride. It could be anyone from a little old lady going to church to a dope dealer going from the east side of Baltimore to the west side. Either way, it was five, ten, or twenty dollars. And sometimes when it was a dealer, you got to cut out the money and get the dope right then and there. This just so happened to be how I got the dope the day I overdosed under that bridge.

That is the thing with buying heroin—you never know how pure it is, and you are playing Russian Roulette every time you stick that needle in your arm. I left from that situation under the I-95 bridge and didn't stop. I was on a path that would eventually lead to the point of sure death if I kept going.

As I write this, I am overwhelmed with a feeling of gratitude that I found recovery at the time that I did, because I would certainly be a statistic in the group of people who have fatally overdosed. Back then, fentanyl was not so prevalent as it is now. Had fentanyl been in the heroin I took all of those years ago, I certainly would have died. There is no question about it!

Why Joey and Not Me?

In May, 2001, I got the news that my dear friend Joey had died. I was at someone's apartment getting high. I was a fugitive from justice in the Texas system for a possession of heroin charge and a new assault charge in Maryland. Now the police were looking for me.

My ex-girlfriend Mary called me and said, "Joey is dead." It hit me right between the eyes, and it hurt badly. Not only was he dead, but he and I'd had a falling out a few months back and hadn't talked in a while. Honestly, Joey was tired of me and concerned about my life, and like a lot of people, he had been worried I was going to end up dead.

He was also good friends with Mary and was put in a position of loving me as a friend and her as well. And let's just say I was a complete jerk to Mary. I did some horrible things to her, from stealing stuff from her to cheating on her while she was out of town once. Joey knew a lot of this stuff and told her. In his defense, the only reason it came out was because I was missing one time in Mary's car and they were looking for me.

Anyway, when I got the news, I freaked out! I was staying with a girl I was using with and I was in and out of her house all the time. Well, the day of Joey's funeral I was getting dressed, and there was a knock at the door.

My girlfriend went to the door and said, "Who is it?"

They replied, "Howard County Sheriff's Department, Warrant Squad. We are looking for Timothy Dale Weber."

"He is not here," she said.

I was in the bedroom and heard it all. I ran through the back door in my boxers and dress socks and made it out across the back of the apartments to my car, which I had parked two complexes over for just this situation. Needless to say, they were not leaving. I kept calling from a pay phone and asking if they were gone.

"No, they are parked out front," she told me.

Finally, I called Mary and told her, and she let me come out to her house. So I missed the viewing, funeral, and everything because I was afraid they would go there looking for me. I still regret that to this day. I often wondered back then how Joey could die. He had everything going for him. He was not nearly as bad off with drugs as me, and he was, bright, good-looking, and could do anything. Why him and not me?

I stayed at Mary's to hide out basically. I was a mess. I was sick from not having any dope and didn't stay long, maybe a day or so. Then, I took off and was back in the city getting high.

At this point, I was literally running out of places to hide, so I ended up running to Pennsylvania with a girl that I used to get high with in Maryland. She had moved there and was more than willing to let me stay with her. We had a very sick relationship, and we fed off of each other's diseases so much. I really cleaned up a little bit while I was in Pennsylvania. At least I was only drinking for a while. But as I said earlier, if you are an addict, you can only quiet the storm for a while. It is always brewing up in you, ready to explode. It was just too crazy there, and if I am being honest, I probably wanted to use heroin and didn't even know it. I sure didn't know where to score there. So I left.

I don't know where she is today, but I do pray she has found recovery somewhere. I stayed with her only two or three weeks and then decided I wanted to come back to Maryland. I didn't even tell her I was leaving. I just snuck out of her house early one morning and left, leaving half my clothes there.

My Guardian Angel

I called my dad and asked him to pick me up halfway between Pennsylvania and Maryland. And of course, he did. I am sure I told him I was clean, and technically, I was. When I got home, he said my brother Mike was there and needed help moving his old girlfriend's stuff out of his basement. Well, I was in no mood for this, but I had no choice. I was at their mercy. After all, I knew I had to play the game to get what I wanted. I was back at Dad's with no job, no car, and no plans.

I told my brother I would help with one load and that was it. But that all changed because my brother's ex was bringing a friend to help. Well, when I saw her, my heart dropped. The friend was tall with brown hair, brown eyes, and the most incredible smile. She also had the shape and curves of a supermodel. My attitude quickly changed, and I was willing to move as many loads as needed. Her name was Kathy, and she was most definitely my guardian angel. We spent that day moving and then went our separate ways.

I was trying at this time to stay clean, and I was even going to meetings at the Alono Club in Columbia. I knew if my brother's ex had anything to do with it, this girl wouldn't give me a second thought. She had told her, "He is trouble. Big trouble. You don't want to have anything to do with him."

Well, a few days later, they asked to take Mike and me to lunch for our efforts in the move. I jumped at this opportunity and went. I had started a job at an equipment rental place in Catonsville, Maryland, so I was looking like I was trying, and I am very loveable when I am clean and sober (at least I think so). It was that day that I found out she had been thinking of me as much as I had been thinking of her.

Kathy was a college graduate and working for a major accounting firm. I was a drug addict making nine dollars an hour and renting a room somewhere. Not the best catch in the world, you might say. We ended up going out on a date to see the Baltimore Orioles play, and we talked the whole game and didn't even see one at bat.

It was soon after, maybe two weeks, when I disappeared and went to the city and started using heroin again. I had told her at one point very early on that I was subject to disappear at any given moment. And sure enough, I did.

I want to digress to share how cunning and baffling this disease is. At this point, I was merely abstaining from drinking and drugging, but not doing anything to treat the disease of addiction.

So one day at work, I was going through a co-worker's toolbox and found an old prescription bottle of Percoset pills. I was tempted, to say the least. Sure enough, I tried to "will away" the thought. As anyone familiar with addiction knows, that's impossible when you have not treated the root cause of your addiction.

So I took two Percoset pills one day and by the end of the week, I had taken up to 25 of those pills. I found myself replacing the missing pills with over-the-counter Excedrin tablets. I scraped the letter "E" off the pill, to not give it away. I didn't want anyone to notice that the pills were gone.

This is an example of the means, the opportunity and the desire, all coming together at once if you're not in a recovery program. The means, the opportunity, and the desire to drug or drink is overpowering. The end outcome is always the same—users go back to using.

An important side note: Really, what recovery does for many people like me is that it removes the desire, which is the most important part of the equation.

But recovery was not in sight for me yet. After I took all of those Percosets, I got hooked on heroin, once again.

At that time, during which I disappeared, it was for about three days. When I returned to the room I was renting from a guy, no one was home, so I just went in like nothing was wrong. But I was soon awakened by my dad, the police, and my roommate, and I was asked to leave.

My dad took the keys to the car he had let me use, the guy took his keys to the house, and there I was with nowhere to go. I called Kathy, and she picked me up and drove me around for hours. We ended up at a motel, and I still don't know where that was. I was really coming off heroin badly, and I was sweating so much that night that I soaked the sheets with perspiration. Kathy stayed in the other bed and said she watched me jump, shake, and moan all night.

The next morning, she said she had to take me somewhere, and it wasn't going to be her house. So I chose Howard County General Hospital. I knew I could go in there and tell them I was suicidal and they would have to keep me for seventy-two hours. This is a trick all hard-core addicts have used at some point in their addictions. I got to Howard County General, went in, and said I was going to kill myself. They took me back, and I said goodbye to Kathy. That was a very bad feeling. I really figured it would be the last time I would see her.

I got through my seventy-two hours and was released. My dad picked me up, and I was out and in another room for rent right away. I got another car from my dad and was seeing Kathy again and really giving recovery a try (well…as much as someone who has not been allowed to hit bottom can be trying.)

I want to take a minute to say this: My dad, God love him, wanted nothing more than for me to have a happy life. He tried so hard to do whatever he thought was right to help me, but he could never truly help me until he took the advice of others and let me fall. That meant doing whatever it took to not enable me. I know it was hard on him, and he had many sleepless nights wondering if his youngest son was dead or alive. Ultimately, I think his enabling me is a true sign of his guilt from what happened with my mom and with my childhood.

Being a father myself, I can empathize with him today. I would probably make the same mistakes he had with the enabling. But I do know this: the only way to love and help an addict is to let him or her fall, and fall hard. I am not saying don't help at all, but under no circumstances bail them out for years like my dad did.

Okay, back to the addict. I was working at a candy vending services place and seeing Kathy. As long as I was clean, Kathy would see me, and when I would get off track, she would distance herself from me. She loved me from afar and prayed her heart off!

I was using soon after I was released from Howard County General. It was around this time that Kathy and her family were heading on a vacation to St. Barth's. I was asked to stay at Kathy and her brother's house and watch it and the cat. Remember, at this time, everyone thought I was clean. But in reality, I had started dabbling again in my drugs, not quite hooked with a bad habit yet but well on my way.

This was in July, 2003. It would be five more months of hell before I allowed God to intervene and my life was saved. I had Kathy's Jeep, and as soon as she left and got on the plane, I was in Baltimore and did not stop for weeks. She came back, I think, seven days later, and I was to pick her up at the airport, but I was nowhere to be found. During her trip we did talk on the phone, and I, of course, acted like everything was fine. This again shows how powerful this drug addiction can be. I knew she was coming home that day. I got up at her and her brother's house sicker than a dog. By now, I was hooked again after seven straight days of shooting speedballs. I even stole her brother's change and a lot of DVDs to get high. I really hope all this is hitting someone hard, because this is the truth about addiction. It turns normal, good people into monsters and animals who will do anything to anyone at any time in order to feed their addictions. I knew full well that they would know I took this stuff, and I didn't care—well, I did, but my disease didn't.

I hurt and embarrassed Kathy so much by not showing up at the airport to pick her up. Because her family was traveling in a group, they were with her at the airport waiting for me to give Kathy a special ride home as a couple. Imagine her mom, dad and siblings all there, expecting me to give Kathy a ride to her brother's place. Her family already knew my history and they probably thought: "We guess he's using again."

When she eventually got home with her brother, the house looked like they had been robbed, and in essence they had. Not only that, but I had her car, and I stayed gone for another few days.

I was in Baltimore, and she had not heard from me yet, so she came looking for me. She found me. I saw her pull up, and I had just done a shot of dope five minutes earlier. When I saw her, I thought I was going to pass out.

She pulled up to me, looked me in the eye, and said the most loving thing someone could have ever said to me. "Tim, you are a good man, and you deserve better," she said with the saddest look in her eyes.

I remember feeling as low as someone could feel at that moment. I figured that the least I could do is to tell her where I left her Jeep, since I had used it the whole time she was on vacation. I didn't even help her get back to her car. No, I simply assumed that she found the Jeep, got in to it, and drove away.

A couple of days later, I had another overdose on Washington Boulevard. I had done a shot and walked out of the abandoned house I was visiting, and I blacked out again.

I woke up, once again, to police and paramedics. They shot me full of NARCAN®. Also, when I woke up, I looked into the street, and standing in the middle of the road was Kathy. As plain as day, I saw her looking at me. I even told the paramedics my girlfriend was going to drive me home. Was I hallucinating or was it real? Was it a fog from overdosing or did she rush back to my side?

They asked, "Where is she?" and I pointed to the street. They said there was no one there.

I looked again and she was gone. I went to a pay phone and called her. As an aside, many people may not remember the days of paying for a phone call with coins. She told me that she had not been there at all. I know in my heart she was watching over me in spirit and in prayer.

A few days later, I went back to my room, and Kathy came by to check on me. Meanwhile, my dad was obtaining a court order to have me picked up on a protective custody order, which is granted when you are a danger to yourself or others. And I was. I wanted to die, and I could have killed someone any time I drove. Sometime, later that day, I was picked up by the police and taken to Howard County General on a court order.

When you are taken into the hospital for a court order, they take your clothes and put you in a hospital gown. After a few hours, I was tired of waiting on a doctor to come evaluate me, and I was not feeling very well from not having any dope. I was well on the verge of getting dope sick soon. So, I ran out the emergency room door in my gown— no underwear and no shoes. I made it maybe a block. The police had been called and it was that quick. I was handcuffed and brought back to the hospital, and a guard was posted outside the door of my room.

The doctor came in. He was a psychiatrist I had seen many times before from when I voluntarily came in to eat and clean up for three days. He said, "I have no choice but to commit you, Tim. You're going to be sent to Springfield Hospital."

This was a lockdown facility in Sykesville, Maryland. I got there around three in the morning and slept till around ten the next morning.

When I woke up, I was in a place where there were people with serious and chronic mental health disorders. Not only did some have substance use issues, but add to that, mental health disorders, as well.

Looking back, I was just as sick as the other people there, who were seeing and hearing things and thought they were turning into lizards. But how sick was I? That was yet to be determined.

Back to the lizards—one guy just wouldn't believe that he wasn't turning into one. You couldn't tell him any different.

Was I just like him, but with different symptoms? I kept doing the same thing over and over again, expecting different results. I was probably thirty-six years old at this time, and I knew every time I took a drink of alcohol, I would end up using drugs, going to jail, becoming homeless, and losing everything, yet I continued to do it. So who was more affected—me or the lizard man?

Well, to show you the depths to which we will go in order to continue using drugs and fight recovery, listen to this craziness. As I share the next part of the story, keep in mind that I am at a lockdown psychiatric hospital, which makes my next move very dramatic—almost like mystery movie material.

I noticed it took three seconds for the door to close after someone walked through it, so I watched a nurse walk through, and then I made my way to the door and put my foot in the doorway. I looked behind me. No one saw me, so out the door I went. When patients got to this hospital, they were able to get dressed in their street clothes, so I was dressed and now in the corridor. I needed to get out of another locked door. Addicts are very intuitive, and I knew I could get out.

I walked the long hallway, found a nurse on the other end, and said, "Hi, I was here visiting my brother, and I got locked in. Could you please let me out?"

She answered, "Sure, sir," and opened the door.

I was free. Now that I was out of the locked area, I still had to figure out where the heck I was. I walked into the security office and went right up to an officer.

"Sir, I was up here visiting my brother, and my car won't start. Could you give me a ride up to the High's store?" I had heard people talking about a High's convenience store up the road during my short stay.

He said, "Sure, buddy. No problem."

Okay, so now I was completely off the grounds. Next, I just had to get home with no money and no car. I asked someone who was walking into the store if he could give me a ride to Howard County. I have no idea why, but he did. And there I was—home—probably twenty-four hours after being picked up by the police and escaping from two places. I lay in my bed. All was well in Tim's world.

I called Kathy and gave her some crazy story. I think I told her they let me out early to go to a rehab or something, so I asked her to stop by. I didn't know it, but the hospital called her soon after and said I escaped. She told them I was home. So, the same police who had originally picked me up were back at my house and returned me to Springfield, where I spent two weeks.

The end was nearing. I had two doctors there who would not let me get away with anything. They were great. I didn't think so then, but looking back, I know they played a huge part in my recovery. I still stop by Springfield to this day and let them know I am doing well and what I am up to.

Part 2

What Happened to Change Me

The Look That Changed My Life

Every addict must hit bottom. Here is mine. I had been in a halfway house in Baltimore and had about thirty days clean and sober. Kathy was happy, my family was happy, and I thought I was on my way this time. I was going to meetings and doing the right thing. I had a job and was really trying.

Well, this is another example of how powerful and insidious this disease is. I was out on my pass, and Kathy and I went to visit a friend of hers. The friend's boyfriend was an active addict, and I was thirty days clean and sober. Kathy was so proud of me. The girl's boyfriend asked me to give him a ride to the store to steal something. He came out and then asked me to give him a ride to sell it in the city.

I can't believe I did this. I had no plans to use, but he went into a house, and I knew he was in there shooting coke. After about ten minutes, I went in and could not resist. I had a needle in my arm within minutes. I did not go back to the girl's house to pick up Kathy, and she had to find a ride home.

Understand this: this guy's girlfriend did not use drugs, and Kathy surely had nothing to do with drugs. They were just both caught in the middle of two disgusting addicts. Kathy found out later that her friend had lied to her about her boyfriend. She had told Kathy he had been clean and sober for close to a year, so Kathy had thought he would be a good person for me to be around.

I finally came back to the house. Kathy was back over there, waiting on me. She was furious! She yelled, she screamed, and really let me have it. We ended up leaving together, and the next day she gave me a ride back out to their house to pick up my dad's truck. We had talked all night, and I was supposed to go into a long-term rehab the next day.

That very next day, I still had money in my pocket, and when she dropped me off, I had something else in mind. We headed out, her in her Jeep behind me and me in my dad's truck. When we got to the road where I should have gone in one direction to head to the rehab, I didn't.

I went towards Baltimore. She saw this. I could see her in my rear-view mirror and I caught her giving me a look that saved my life. A look of shame, disgust, and fear. A look that said, *"How could you do this to me, your kids, and everyone who loves you?*

It was a look—as you have read throughout this book—I had grown accustomed to. However, this time it hit me like a ton of bricks. This was the first time in my life that God allowed me to feel, I mean really feel, some emotions. They were intense, and I saw the same look I had caused in all the people who loved me all the way to Baltimore.

It was the same look my son gave me one day when he was four or five and had a basketball in his hand and wanted to shoot some hoops with him. He said, "Dad, please don't go!" I told him I would be back soon. And, he replied, "No you won't. You never come back when you leave." And he was right.

I also thought of another time I was supposed to take my kids and nieces to Six Flags. I left on a Friday and didn't come home until Monday. My brother had come and picked his kids up, and when I walked in the house, my little blond-haired daughter, Megan, was at the door. She gave me that look of shame and disgust that said, *"What have I done to deserve a father like you?* She was probably twelve at that time, and she was mad and hated me for years for that.

The negative ripple effect of my using caused abandonment and childhood trauma in my children (who are now grown adults) that may have contributed to their own addictions, which they have overcome over time. Back in their early years, there were so many broken promises, not just that one particular event. Another time, my grandmother died, and I took all our money and was behind the Cotton Bowl in Dallas, shooting dope through the whole funeral. I finally emerged days later and saw that same look on everyone's face. In every one of these situations, drugs had been more important to me than anything.

I thought about all that stuff all the way to the city. And I know this was my intervention from God, because up until this point, I had been cold as ice. I did not feel anything. I might have acted like it at times, but I didn't. I could make a tear show up in the corner of my eye at the right time when needed to get what I wanted, but this was different. I was all alone. It was just me and God in that car, and it hurt, badly. I had no money, so I continued to the city and got high. But it did not work. I was high, but I could not get those feelings out of my head. This was sometime around November 6, 2003.

November 8, 2003

On November 8, 2003, I walked into Howard County General and said I was going to kill myself once again. They took me back, and I saw one of the same doctors I had seen since forever doing this bit.

She looked at me and said, "Tim, you are not going to kill yourself. You are an addict and an alcoholic, and we can't help you here anymore."

I looked at her with the most desperate and serious look I ever had. *"Please, please! I am begging you!"* I screamed. "You are right. I am probably not going to kill myself, but I am dying out there, and if you don't help me, I will die or end up in prison for the rest of my life."

Again, God stepped in and had to have touched that doctor, because she did a complete 180 and said, "Okay, Tim, but if you miss one group, go late to dinner, smoke in the bathroom, or do one thing out of line, I will have you kicked out."

So, I entered the hospital, and from that day forward, my life has changed 100 percent. I did everything in there I was supposed to do. I was at group on time and cleaned up other people's trays after dinner. I mean I was the perfect resident. I called the halfway house I had been in a month earlier, and they said I could come back. I left Howard County General and entered the halfway house with a new attitude. I was at the point when every addict must want recovery and not just need it.

The halfway house was a run-down row house on Linwood Avenue in Baltimore, not five blocks from where I used to score dope. The thing is, it doesn't matter where you are when you are ready to receive God and recovery. It is an inside job.

I linked up with a group of guys at the house who were serious about God and recovery. I got a sponsor in my 12-Step group, and I started to work the steps toward recovery. It was very hard. For the first time I was exposed to every feeling and emotion in the world. I made Kathy crazy with all my insecurities and jealousies. I had known I had all of this, but I had been able to keep it at bay with the drugs and alcohol. Now those were gone. I now asked her everywhere we went, "Do you want that guy? Why were you looking at him?" Why this? Why that? I was crazy. And I never thought I could let people know I was that way. But trust me, there are a lot of people out there that way, especially addicts. We feel so bad about ourselves that we don't know what to do.

Thankfully, at this point in my life, I can tell you what I did. I stayed sober and worked through the 12 Steps and became a productive member of society. I got a job and started catching a bus in Baltimore to work. I made six dollars an hour pulling staples at some kind of insurance records place. I literally made enough money to catch a bus for a week, pay my hundred dollars a week rent, and maybe buy a hamburger at a fast-food place. But I was doing it all on my own, and I was feeling really good about that.

After a few months there, I got another job at a flower shop in the city. I made nine dollars an hour and was able to eventually get a car, through the help of my father and my house manager, who was selling it. I was really feeling good. I was praying every day, going to meetings, and working. Kathy was coming around, and a little trust was building with my family as well. I had made a commitment to stay in the halfway house for six months and then discuss leaving with my sponsor.

Part 3
What It Is Like Today

Cattails Country Florist

Sometime around April 2004, Kathy and I were taking a friend of mine to a meeting. When we dropped him off, his dad came out and gave me a newspaper clipping of a flower shop for sale in Woodbine, Maryland. I had told him on a number of occasions that I would like to own a flower shop again one day when the time was right. Well, who knew the time would be when I was living in a recovery house with only six months clean and sober! But again, God will bless you wherever you are, and only He knows when the time is right.

Kathy said, "Call the number. You know you want to."

I replied, "Kathy, they probably want way too much money. And let's not forget, I live in a halfway house and make nine dollars an hour."

Well, let me just say this: all things are possible with God on your side. So, I called, and they wanted a reasonable amount of money for it. Now understand, if they wanted two hundred dollars for it, that was about one hundred and ninety-eight dollars short of what I had. But again, all things are possible. At this time Kathy was working in Virginia for an accounting firm, making a lot more money than nine dollars an hour. The thought of us buying a flower shop together seemed a little bit crazy—that is, to everyone but us. We had figured out a way to buy the shop the week of Mother's Day and pay for it with the money we made that week. I knew that if they really made the sales they had shown us, this was possible.

We took over the shop on May 1, 2004, and did exactly what we had planned. The shop was paid off after that first week. We moved to Sykesville, Maryland, around the time we bought the shop. Ironically, it was located right across the street from Springfield Hospital. We still had to have extra money to operate and live, and it just kept coming in. God provided everything we needed.

The first year was very tough. We slept on the floor many times and had many sleepless nights. We started growing slowly, we both kept God first, and kept my recovery my number-one priority. So, there we were, me six months sober and Kathy leaving a job she had a degree for. I know she was scared, but she had faith. As for me, there was nowhere to go but up. As for her, she could leave a job that had all the benefits and the pay which big companies offer—and possibly lose it all.

But it was working and time rolled on. My first-year (clean and sober) anniversary arrived on November 8, 2004. I had been planning this event since the first day I got sober. This time I had invited everyone I knew to my first-year anniversary, and it was wonderful. All my family, Kathy's family, and all my friends in and out of meetings were there. I had planned my speech for a whole year, but I ended up saying nothing like I had planned.

Will You Marry Me, Again?

After my one-year anniversary, I planned to propose to Kathy. This would be the second time I had proposed. The first time was right before she went to Saint Barth's, and it was not a good situation. She did say yes, the first time, but we never set a date. In fact, she called it off soon after she returned from St. Barth's, and I am sure you understand why. She had told me she would not even consider marrying me unless I was a year clean and sober.

It was a year that night, and I was ready to ask her again under much better circumstances. I ordered three hundred and sixty-five red roses, took them to our apartment, and spread them all over the living room and bedroom. There was one rose for every day I was clean and sober.

We came home from my celebration, and when we got to the house, Kathy opened the door and said, "Oh my God, what happened in here?"

If you didn't know what you were looking at, that many roses looked like someone had ransacked our house. After she realized they were roses, she went to the bedroom, and on her pillow lay one white rose with the ring tied to it. She picked it up, and I got on my knee and asked, "Will you marry me?"

She replied, "Yes." Then she asked, "What is the white rose for?"

I told her it was to signify that the ring was no longer tainted and was pure, and that my motives were pure. So, we started planning our wedding for August 21, 2005.

Our first year at the shop came and went, and we were really growing, so much so that it was becoming impossible for us to keep up with all our business. Thanks in part to my good friends at the funeral home, Jim and Todd, we had started a deal on linking our websites, and we just exploded with funeral business. This is when we met Mandy, our head designer and manager. She walked in looking for a job, and we hired her soon after. She has been such a blessing and is the best designer and friend in the world.

Her hiring freed me up to deliver and market our business and for Kathy to learn more hands-on stuff at the shop. Things just kept getting better at the shop, and we eventually hired a full-time driver so I could help Mandy with designing. Kathy turned into quite the astute florist. She is the best wedding consultant around in my opinion. It is hard to say no to her and her infectious, happy-go-lucky personality.

Our wedding was soon upon us, and let me tell you, we were excited. My son was my best man, and my daughter was my best lady. Kathy's brother was her "man of honor" or, as I called him, her "dude of honor." Everyone was there, and it was a wonderful day. I will never forget it and will cherish it forever. My son's toast to Kathy left not one dry eye in the room:

Guardian Angel
by Michael Dale Weber-August 21, 2005
God works in mysterious ways.
You are here, and I am glad you are here to stay.

Your spirit soars like a dove.
When I see you and Dad, I know that it's true love.

You make my dad happy, and I can see.
You are the best that can be.

When I see y'all, I know it's faith.
I can tell by the smile you put on my dad's face.

You got my dad out of twists and tangles;
You are truly my dad's guardian angel.

My brother-in-law's and father-in-law's toasts topped the night off. It was one of the best nights of my life to this day.

We went to the Bahamas for our honeymoon, and it was amazing. While there, I thought that less than two years ago I had been a homeless drug addict, and there I was on the beach in the Bahamas. How cool was that? God is great!

Super Bowl XLI

Super Bowl XLI—the Super Bowl. I will never forget despite the fact I didn't see on first down. This was the day my daughter woke up from her coma after having an emergency liver transplant. Five months earlier she had given birth to my grandson, Nicholas. She was driving home from work one day, swerved to miss a deer, and flipped her car. After one month of being laid up with a broken back, she went into liver failure from the pain medication, both over-the-counter and prescribed.

When I got the hospital, she was given seventy-two hours to live. I was in shock! I tried to hold it together, but I must admit I lost it a few times. I did not use drugs or drink during this period, but I surely acted like the old Tim a time or two. To make matters worse, Megan and I had not been speaking at the time, and I had not talked to her in over a month. This was a mistake on both our parts. We are both hard-headed and headstrong. Neither of us would give in.

When I walked to Johns Hopkins and saw her, all of that fell by the wayside. I just wanted my little girl to live. It was not looking good. She was third on the transplant list, and the hours were ticking away. I flew my son, Michael, up from Texas, where he was living. He was nineteen at the time and her best chance for a live donor match. You can take part of a good liver and put it in someone else, and both halves will grow and work.

We had so many people test to be donors. Even the doctors at Johns Hopkins said it was unbelievable how many people tried to support us. And I must say that a good majority of them were from my recovery meetings. Recovering addicts and alcoholics, when in recovery, are some of the most caring and loving human beings in the world.

As it turned out, no one was a perfect match except Michael. So the doctor went over the procedure, and Michael signed all the paperwork. The plan was to have them in surgery the next morning. He was so brave and really wanted to help his sister. I, on the other hand, was not so brave. I was really scared to lose both of them. I prayed, Kathy prayed, Kathy's mom prayed. Let's just say everyone from here to Texas was praying his or her heart out.

The next morning Michael had an IV in his arm, and we were getting ready to walk him down to the operating room.

But then the doctor walked in and said, "Mr. Weber, we found a liver. It is in Puerto Rico, and I am getting on a plane in half an our to go get it."

We were so relieved. Our prayers were answered. Now let me say this: the doctors at Johns Hopkins were fabulous. They never once gave us false expectations, yet they always made us comfortable. I mean, who would ever think that the head of the liver department at the hospital would actually fly all that way and check the liver out, bring it back, and assist in putting it in Megan? Talk about going above and beyond the call of duty. I know they would probably do this for anyone, but they sure made us feel special, and we had all the confidence in the world in them.

The liver went in on February 2, 2007, and on February 4, Super Bowl Sunday, I was standing next to Megan as she lay in the hospital, on a ventilator to breathe for her. There was a small twitch in her hand.

You have to understand that for close to a week there had been nothing, no sign of life at all, so this gave us some needed hope.

A few hours later, I was back in there next to her, and all of a sudden, her eyes opened. I screamed, *"Oh my God! She is awake!"* I ran down the hallway to the waiting room and yelled, *"She is up. My God, she is awake!"*

From that point on, it was up and down. She slowly started talking through her ventilator, and the first words she mouthed to me were, "Dad, I am sorry, and I love you."

I thought I was going to die right there. It killed me that we had let things go on for so long. I made a promise right then and there to never let petty things come between me and the people I love. You never know what can happen from one day to another.

We spent close to a year in and out of the hospital, and we had many trying days, but God was with us, and we made it. I am happy to say Megan is doing great, is working at a local pediatrician's office, and taking care of her son, Nicholas.

God, Meetings, Service and Family

Today, I am clean and sober and go to at least three meetings a week. I pray every day. I have a sponsor. I have a home group and I am active in helping others who are lost in this disease of addiction. I volunteer with different groups throughout my community and try to get this message out to anyone who will listen.

I have served on the Carroll County Behavioral Health and Addiction Planning Committee. I have also gone through a program called Choices to become an instructor for kids who have minor violations with the law that range from alcohol citations to misdemeanor drug charges. I have been a Maryland Director of In the Blink of an Eye Ministries, which is a nonprofit organization to help addicts and families of addicts in their quests for recovery. I have met some of the best people in the world on my journey in recovery. My life is filled with such peace and serenity today. I am so grateful for every breath I take. I was so lost for so long. I now try to take advantage of every second of every day.

I hope this gives you a little insight into what drug addicts go through and what they put everyone else through. We are not bad people. We are sick, and like any other sickness, we must be treated. I found, for me, the only treatment that worked is a relationship with God and the 12-Step recovery program I am involved with. Because of this treatment, I am now one of those people walking to the football game in a Raven's jersey.

I am a good father, son, husband, brother, friend, and oh yeah, a grandfather today. I am a respected member of my community and have friends from the state's attorney's office, Maryland State Police, local police departments, churches, and more. I have a life today beyond my wildest dreams, and I will never forget where I came from. So, when I see someone homeless on the street, I pray that he or she meets the God I met and will be led out of his or her despair. I know everyone knows someone who needs to hear a message of hope and that there is a way out, just like I heard many years ago.

It took a long time for me to move out of the way and let God take over, but now that I have, all things are possible. My wife and I own and operate a very successful flower shop and we own a home. We live just a few houses down from my wife's parents, and they have become two of our best friends. We have done so many fun things together like paintball games, scuba diving, hiking, and just hanging out watching football games. The father I feared so much is one of my best friends and golf buddies. We try to play golf once a week during the golf season with my two brothers, who are both in recovery as well. Let me tell you, out of all I have today, the most important thing to me is the peace I have on a daily basis. I wake up every day without a guilty conscience, and that is worth a million dollars!

Part 4
The Story of the Weber Sober Homes

Fear Turns into an Idea

I was driving down the road in Westminster, Maryland, in late December, 2008 after what appeared to be a successful Christmas at our flower shop. I was pondering some big orders we had not gotten. What had started out as a good, accomplished feeling was quickly overtaken by fear. That is what we addicts do in and out of recovery. The difference in being in recovery versus not being in recovery is that we try to find a remedy to the fear as opposed to covering it up.

My mind was all over the place with worry. I thought of what we (my wife and I) would do if we lost or had to close the shop. My wife, Kathy, is good and level-headed. She graduated from South Carolina with an accounting degree, and until she met me, she was well on her way to a successful accounting career.

Kathy comes from a long line of accountants (her father and uncle, both successful). And in my opinion, Kathy is the most intelligent woman I know. While the shop is her love and passion, she could easily make money doing something in her degree field.

All I know is flowers. And unless you own a shop, you really don't make enough money to support a family. There are other areas in the flower business you can go, but even those jobs require a degree. I spent, as you know from earlier chapters, most of my life in and out of rehab centers, jails, and homeless shelters. I did graduate high school, but if I am being honest, I stopped paying any attention in school in the sixth grade, soon after my mother died. It's no excuse, but that is what I recall. My manipulation and playing the death of a parent card got me a long way. In fact, I have no idea how I graduated high school. In other words, I manipulated my way through school. Add all this to my work history (or lack thereof) and a criminal past, and you can see where I might be a bit fearful.

Actually, I was scared to death that I was not good enough to do anything else. I knew if I applied for a job, my past would be discovered. I didn't think anyone would trust me, respect me, or give me a chance. As an addict in recovery, I had respect in my community, but as an employee, I wasn't so sure. To some people, addicts can never change. Some people think, "once an active addict, always an active addict." This view kept me down for years. I believed that lie. I am on a mission to let everyone know we *can* and *do* change, and we *can* lead honest productive lives. Some of the most trustworthy people I know are recovered addicts in the program. Our textbook tells us clearly that we do recover.

So, you can see where my fear about finding something else to do came from. Having said all this, we had just completed a successful year at the shop, and we were not about to lose it in any shape, form, or fashion. It was just an addict creating some fear that in all actuality was about to lead to good things and a win–win endeavor.

"What would I do if?" was my dilemma. Well, maybe I could work somewhere in the field of addiction, possibly become a counselor or work in a rehab center. But again, you need a degree and not that damn criminal past! Rats!

At this time, I was five years clean and sober, had just released my book, was speaking at local addiction events, and was really getting involved in Carroll County, Maryland, where my wife and I live.

Out of the blue it came to me: why don't you start a sober/recovery home? There were none in our county, and I was getting calls from people asking for help, and I just directed them to the city where I got sober.

Why not? I knew addiction, and if I did it right, I could really give back what was given to me, supplement my income, and possibly turn it into something I love to do. Down the road, I could possibly make a living doing what I love—helping other people like me.

I also remembered an incident years ago when I was in one of many rehabs. I was in a circle of new guys, talking with them, showing them around, and telling them what to expect there. The owner of the rehab (Isiah) came to me afterward and said, "Tim, you do know this is what you should be doing?" I looked at him like he was crazy. I was in my sixteenth rehab or so, and was really just thinking, *how do I end up in rehab just about every year?*

A month or so later, I was talking to Isiah at the Ranch, and again he said, "Some of us need to be around this all the time—people in recovery struggling, counting on us—and that is how we make it." He went on to say, "Can you imagine all the people I would let down if I used again? My wife, kids, the forty-five guys here on the ranch, and my community." Lastly, he ended with this: "What I have done is surround myself with so much accountability that it, in a sense, protects me. It is not my recovery, but it is most definitely part of my recovery process."

If there is one thing I know for sure, it is that the only way to stay clean, sober, and spiritually connected is through carrying this message to others. That means practicing the steps in my life and taking other people through that same process.

I left that meeting on cloud nine and was eager to do what he did someday.

A few rehabs, overdoses, and arrests later, I hit bottom and got sober.

And just like buying a flower shop at six months sober, five years later we were opening our first sober home!

Weber Sober Homes Begins

After talking things over with my wife and praying about it, we decided to go for it. As an aside, when I am reading this part of the story to my wife, she laughs and says, "That is not at all how it happened, but if that's what you think, oh well." She goes on to say I got the idea, the obsession began, and no one could stop me, not even her.

I will say this: from the flower business to the sober homes, if God is not in it, it will fail. I mean if it is humanly forced for the wrong reason, it is going to fail. I believe this with all my heart. I know this from experience that the inner conscience usually saying no is really God speaking to me. I have tried ideas and adventures through the years that went down quickly! But the flower shop and homes are still standing, thank God!

The first step in the process was determining what we would tell our sober home. After much thought, we came up with a base name: Weber Addiction Group, LLC d/b/a Weber Sober Homes. That way if we decided to open more houses later, we could operate under this. So, now we had the name.

There is a reason I felt it necessary and appropriate to use my family name, Weber.

As you know, prior to getting sober, my name was mud. From the time I was a kid, I was in trouble, and when people heard the name Tim

Weber, they knew it was trouble. I had girlfriends in high school who had to hide the fact that they were going out with me. Good friends' parents cringed when they said they were hanging out with me. It was very upsetting to me, but I never told anyone. Before you spend a second even starting to feel sorry for me, believe me, I deserved the reputation.

As a kid, I skipped school as early as the fourth grade. I even talked some of the other kids into leaving school to hide out at an abandoned church and bust out windows. This was in the fourth freaking grade!

Things only got worse.

In high school, I fought, drank beer, and smoked weed. One time when I was drinking, I got into it with some guys at an after-hours party at school. As always, a fight and a brawl ensued. Of all the people to jump in to help me was my good friend James, who was not a fighter. Well, I jumped in a car with a girl and bolted, thinking the fight was over. I was wrong. We heard from friends soon after that my friend was in the hospital with a broken jaw!

I went to the hospital and was in tears. James' parents came, and they made it clear that they did not want me around at all. In fact, there were a lot of friends who felt this way. So my friend James spent six weeks with his jaw wired shut. Not once did he make me feel bad about it. Just to keep you in touch with this guy from earlier in the book, James is the one who has not spoken to me over an amends I have tried to make for a few years. When we started the Candy Gift Bouquet Company, I had walked out on him. I do understand his feelings and respect them. It is a person's right to not accept our amends. And God knows that before recovery, I had many false amends.

Those are two scenarios of the early years with the Weber name. However, as of November 8, 2003, all that changed after working with a sponsor through the 12-Steps. I am no longer ashamed of the Weber name. In fact, my daughter Megan recently said to me, "Dad, when I get married, I am going to keep my last name." As I am writing this, I can't tell you the joy that gives me.

As you know, this is the same little girl who years ago would not even call me Dad. Megan spent years addicted to pain killers and battled addiction prior to her liver transplant. She shares her story in a powerful way to young people all over Maryland. In 2021, she celebrated her 12 years of being clean and sober.

So, while I am on the subject of the Weber Family, I would like to say how proud I am of my son, Michael. There's more to come later in the book about him….

With all of this goodwill surrounding the Weber name, the decision was made: Weber Sober Homes would be the name. I knew how to start a business, but I am well-known for putting the cart before the horse. I got on the Internet and started looking for rental houses. I found a ton. After all, we were going into the worst recession our country had seen in years with the housing meltdown, so everyone was willing to rent. But would they rent to a guy who wanted to house a bunch of alcoholics and addicts? And, on top of that, a house would need furniture, insurance, corporate documents, money, and let's not forget—guys to join the sober home.

We found a house and we were in. We opened the doors to our first home in January, 2009. I needed an LLC and we decided on the name The Weber Addiction Group, LLC. This name allows us to explore other avenues of help, including intensive outpatient groups (IOP), counseling, etc.

We were looking to fill the home, so I knew where to get at least one bed, two couches, a TV, and some dishes. But I knew my wife would probably not be too happy. She was shocked when she looked into our spare bedroom and basement. She thought we had been robbed (so to speak). After she saw it in our sober home and saw how things were coming together, she was okay with it. And I was relieved.

Now that we were open, I had drug tests, alcohol testers, meeting slips, recovery meetings posted on the fridge—all the things the Weber Sober Home needed to start…except *people*!

I was ready to start picking up homeless people off the streets of Westminster, Maryland. I began to wonder, *What the hell have I done?* In trying to help my family and help others, I had loaded us down with more monthly payments.

So, I went back down on my knees, and I am sure my wife did as well, and it hit me—or God hit me. I had been in more rehab centers and hospitals in this area for addiction, and I knew the need for these homes. It started there.

I got my book and some brochures my brother-in-law helped me put together through their printing business, and I pounded the pavement. I went to Howard County General, where prior to getting sober, I had run out half-naked to escape their psychological evaluation. I went to all the places I had frequented in my attempts at getting sober and gave them a book and a brochure.

Through a friend of mine, a counselor, we got our first resident. His name was Matt. Within the next couple of days, I got a call from Howard County General, and resident number two, Andy, arrived.

As time went on, I got connected with the drug court of Carroll County, the Health Department, and the probation office. The sober home was full before I knew it.

I lived in sober homes on and off through the years, but never realized how much was involved in the venture I had taken on. It was up to me to become a human lie detector, counselor, father, brother, and example to all these guys. And let me tell you, it was and is a learning process. Once I realized I was not in control of anything and God was, it sure made it easier.

As an addict, I tried every way possible to lie in order to continue my drug and alcohol use. In fact, I thought I knew all the tricks. Once

Weber Sober Homes opened, I soon learned that I didn't. The one thing I do know are the desperate and manipulative things we addicts will do to hide and cover our tracks.

I had one guy take a urine drug test. When I dipped the test stick into the cup and pulled it out to read it, I found out the liquid was full of food coloring, and it had dyed the test cartridge. I could not help but laugh at this one. I looked at him and said, "Dude, too much dye. C'mon man, be honest with me, and we can get you clean and let you come back." Well, he got half-honest. He was dirty for opiates, a drug I know too well. But he said (as all heroin addicts do), "Man, I found a Percocet when I went home to get clothes." We always go to pills, like it's better than actual heroin. I am here to tell you it is not!

I decided to share a quick story with this young man. I shared with him that when I was in my active addiction, I once bought food coloring and tried to fool my wife (then girlfriend). Well, I had it all planned out. She did not watch me pee, so I put a bit of yellow coloring in the cup of water, and dipped the test cartridge right in front of her. I was also really hamming it up, saying that if it was anything other than opiates, it was a false positive because I only did dope (heroin).

Well, it came up two lines on everything but freaking opiates (two lines mean clean, one means positive)! I kid you not, water and food coloring showed opiates. I told him, "Now if that was not God doing for me what I needed, I don't know what is."

Now, when I share that story, people find it hard to believe, but it's true. Soon after that, I embarked on the journey of recovery that led me to where I am today.

So, I told him he had to pack up and leave for now, and that if he would get clean, I would give him a chance to come back. I am sad to say I have not heard from him. I can only hope he made it back into recovery somewhere.

The Joey V. House

The original Weber Sober Home opened and was soon full! I had no intention of opening a second house, but God had other plans. As I said, I was getting involved in my county's efforts to fight our addiction problems. While I was on the Behavioral Health and Addictions Planning Committee, another person attending a meeting said to me one day, "Tim, come with me after the meeting." She took me to this beautiful brick house in a good area and told me, "I'm renting this out and wondered if you would be interested." Shocked, I said I needed to talk to my wife to see what she thought.

I knew what my plans were. Yes! I had one house full and was already turning people away. Kathy and I went to see the brick house inside and out, and we said yes.

"What are you going to call this one?" my wife asked. I already knew the answer: The Joey V. House after my best friend from high school who died of this disease one year before I got clean and sober. After writing the first edition of this book, I hooked up with Joey's family, and they read it. I had not used Joey's real name. Joey's aunt said, "Tim, you know Joey or us would not care if you use his name in your book." In fact, she went on to say, "Joey would rather have his name than your fictitious name of Toby."

I totally got that because if you knew Joey, he was never too shy for the limelight. So, I approached his family to get permission to name the second sober home after him. It was a resounding *"Yes!"* We would love it." Not only that but they came to see the house, and after many tears from all of us, they approved. So, also in 2009, we opened the Joey V. Sober Home.

By this time, I was doing a lot of work with the court system and getting referrals from court and jail as well as hospitals and treatment centers. I must say we have one of the best counties for reaching out and trying to help addicts and alcoholics.

Our drug court is top-notch here in Carroll County, Maryland. The judge, Health Department, and the whole team care immensely about helping those who suffer from this disease and understanding it.

Currently, we have two sober homes, and the Joey V. House is the nicer of the two. If you knew Joey, you would know that he would not have it any other way. I decided to have the main office there, and it is the main hub for the houses. We have all meetings there, including parent groups, support meetings, and many other events. I can hear Joey saying, "How ya liking me now?" every time I sit in that house with seven guys looking for a new way of life. And if I have told one Joey story, I've told a thousand.

Luke's Sunrise House

Not even two months after the Joey V. House opened, the *same* person who rented the house to me came back to me and asked, "Tim, can you take a ride with me?" I thought, *she has another house, and there is no way I can do this. Two is enough.* Well, that was before I found out it was four doors down from the Joey V. House!

So, now I had a dilemma. We already had two houses, and we had been offered a third. As I was driving home, I prayed and thought, *Okay, God, is this right? Is it too much? Am I spreading myself thin?* Okay, maybe I was deep in question, not thought. I pulled into my garage, walked through the door, smiled at my wife, and proceeded to say, "Well, I was offered another house."

She replied, "No way, Tim! What you're doing is awesome, and I love the guys, but as it is you are spending more and more time away from the flower shop, not to mention home."

I countered, "Hold on, hold on…You have to hear where it is first. Babe, it's four doors down from the Joey V. House." I could see it in her eyes, and they told me, *He's getting this house.* I said, "Let's at least go look at it together and talk."

We drove over right then because for me there are people who think on and ponder ideas and there are people who pursue ideas. I pursue Squirrel! (This means I am on to a side story). I think much of my putting the cart before the horse mentality comes from wasting thirty-seven years of my life as an addict. I feel like I am a late bloomer in life, so if I am to succeed and retire one day, I have to get busy getting busy.

Most normal people go to college or start a career in their twenties. They settle in, buy a house, start a 401(K), and pay into Social Security. Well, not so much of a retirement plan for a drug addict and alcoholic. From age eighteen to age thirty-seven, if I paid a few thousand dollars into Social Security, it would be an exaggeration because I had not worked, and I have been homeless or in jail, rehabs or shelters the better part of those years. And heck, until I was clean a year or so, I didn't even truly know what a 401(K) was. As you see, I have a bit of ground to make up and I intend to do it.

So, there you have it. The cart before the horse it was once again with the third house. In no way did I start the houses to get rich or make money off of others' misfortunes, because it is my thought that when most of us are ready to get help, we have no money, insurance or even family left to help us. From my experience, my thought is to provide a service through the homes, mentorship, and groups that in return provide me a supplement to my income to help me continue doing it full time one day. It is a win-win for all involved. Even the county and state where these people reside will benefit because we will all be tax-paying contributors to our society and clean and sober. And who knows? Just maybe a few guys will be touched by God, and go out and do the same thing we have done and open a sober home. That, my friends, is worth all the money in the world!

As for my houses, no expense is too much. I regularly pay for drug dogs to sniff all the houses. I use alcohol testers like they are going out of style and drug tests galore, not to mention I only allow outside money to pay a resident's rent for two weeks. The residents then must pay it back. We also sponsor guys with no resources to stay for two weeks free, and they in return pay it back to a sponsorship fund we have. We take no outside funding except an occasional two weeks from drug court, which again is always supposed to be paid back by the individual.

Back to sober home number three. My wife and I sat on the floor of the third house and talked. I said, "Kathy, I am getting more and more calls. I also thought about making the Weber Sober Home (the first house) a three-quarter house."

She looked at me with that beautiful face and a serious look and asked, "So, what are you going to call this house!"

Yes! I thought. *She's in!* The one thing I know for sure is that if Kathy is in agreement, things go much smoother. She is the think-it-through and rational one, not to mention the prayer warrior in my life.

I was thinking Luke's Sunrise. *Luke* was my mom's nickname and *sunrise* came from two of my friends who wanted to have some recovery houses right where we were and call them Sunrise.

That is the story of how the houses came to be.

Soon after, Luke's Sunrise was open, we started having 12-Step recovery meetings at the Joey V. House. We would sit in a circle at the house and hold meetings. After months of wondering what in the world I was doing, I was finally seeing the fruits of our labor as I watched a group of guys sitting around, talking about their problems, opening up, and sharing their lives with us. It really does my heart good. It amazes me to this day as I sit with the guys and realize how far my life has come and how far their lives can go.

Tough Decisions for the Weber Sober Home

Sometime around July, 2009, I made a decision to close the Weber Sober Home after attempting to turn it into a three-quarter house. I realized I was not helping people in the house by doing this. Having the Joey V. and Luke's Sunrise Houses so close, I was there all the time and could give the undivided attention. But for Weber Sober Home, I was neglecting the needed one-on-one time with the guys. Not to mention, that in order to make a three-quarters house work, there needed to be some single rooms.

Also, the house itself was not economically beneficial. It was an old house, and with the rent we paid, AC window units, poor insulation, etc., we decided to close this house before it bled my wife and me dry. My intention was to help us, not cause us to go bankrupt. It became a drain, and until I let it go, we did not feel emotional or financial relief. I knew it was a good idea to eventually have a three-quarters house, but it turned out not to be the right time...yet.

Closing the house was easier said than done. I ended up closing it up and paying out the lease, which was tough with no residents. But all in all, it was the right decision.

So, as of January, 2010, we had the two houses with seven beds in each house, and we were always full.

Start Helping Early!

As guys come into the sober houses, I immediately start taking them around to speak to others about their addictions. We are always involved in speaking engagements at schools, churches, and individual homes to speak to young men who say, "I don't have a problem," just like we all used to say. It occasionally results in interventions, and they go to rehab and come to our house.

A lot of the time they look at us like we are crazy! But if there is one thing I have learned, it is that the spirit hears what the mind does not. In time this kid might be in an abandoned house in Baltimore with a needle in his arm, and that spirit will arise, and through all the fear and pain he is going through, he will remember those guys who told him his life might end up there. Then he will know who to call.

I think some people honestly don't like the way I share my story *all* over. But I know the only reason I came through this nightmare was solely because someone told me the same story years ago. It is essential for me as a recovering addict to reach out and help others, and I pass that on to all the guys who step foot in Weber Sober Homes. Some take heed of it, and others don't. The ones that do, not all but most, will get addicted to helping others, and that is an addiction we all should have!

As time went on at the homes, I noticed we were continuing to have guys stay for nine months to more than a year! I was so happy they were, and the one thing I had always wanted was to never put a time limit on a stay. We don't mess up our lives in six to nine months. Likewise, it can take years to repair correctly—not years to recover but rather years to clean up the wreckage. Once we go through the steps and have a spiritual awakening, and the obsession is removed, we have recovered. It must, however, be nurtured through maintaining that awakening by helping others through the steps—an endeavor I am still going through at the time of this writing, with almost 18 years clean and sober. My problems are much different today, but that past still can interfere with some of the goals I have. So, it is a continual process even now to clean it all up.

Having said that, here we go again. Houston, we have a problem. Guys were staying longer, and with only fourteen beds and my phone ringing incessantly with rehabs, hospitals, and families looking for beds, I wondered, *Do I try that three-quarters house again?* It had been three years since I closed the original house which I had wanted to be a three-quarters house. What to do, what to do?

My son, Michael, and I were driving home from a meeting one night and he asked, "Dad, are you ever going to open another house?" I replied, "Only if something comes up near the Joey V. and Luke's Sunrise Houses. When it is time, I am sure God will open that door. He always has."

Well, I kid you not, that night I got home and opened my e-mail account. Lo and behold there was an email that said, "Mr. Weber, I know what you do over there and was wondering if you were looking for another house?"

Are you kidding me? I thought. I showed my son, and he laughed and said, "Dad, this is crazy." Well, as I said, God would open the door. I guess I just wasn't thinking he would grab me by my hand and pull me right through that door! I am sure this guy had kept an e-mail of mine from a time back when I was looking to start one of the houses. But for it to happen the same day that we were talking about it was most definitely a God deal.

My criteria for doing another house was for it to (a) be close to the others, (b) be affordable, and (c) have enough room for some single rooms.

All three requirements were met, and the three-quarters house was soon in the works. It is located 0.8 miles from the Joey V. House. I made the call, and within one month we were in. I immediately had guys to move in from the other two houses.

The requirements for the three-quarters houses are simple: You must come from the other two houses, be working a good program, follow pretty much the same rules, and definitely stay clean and sober. There is no curfew, which is the draw to the house. They can start having a bit more freedom and see how it goes. If someone breaks rules, he is immediately brought back to the other houses. And trust me, it has been done.

The Stonewall House
Begins in 2012

On August 3, 2011, my cousin Stoney passed away from the effect of the same disease I am afflicted with. My phone rang one morning early. It was my dad.

"Son, your cousin Stoney just died. I am very sorry. I think you should call your Aunt DeDe and Uncle Mike."

Well, I did, and even as I am writing this, I am choking back tears. It was a hard phone call, and I hadn't talked to them in years. We had a long conversation with occasional tearful laughs, and we ended it with "I love you" and planned to talk when services were arranged.

As a strange coincidence, we were having our second annual Joey V. Memorial Golf Tournament on the same day as Stoney's funeral. This tournament honors the namesake of the Joey V. House and helps raise awareness of a growing addiction problem in our country. My family discussed that my two brothers and I would stay to keep the tournament going, and my dad and stepmom would go to the funeral. After all, the Joey V. golf tournament was to raise awareness of the problem of drugs and alcohol. My cousin's family was all for us staying and carrying on the message. So, there you have it. We decided to name our three-quarter house after my cousin Stoney. His nickname growing up had been Stonewall, so the Stonewall House it became.

Having the sober houses has opened so many doors to not only me, but also to many others. We have guys who are moving on to be counselors, executives, construction workers, and maybe even future sober home owners. But, most importantly they are guys who are being fathers, sons, brothers, and honest, productive tax-paying members of our community.

The Blessings of Life

If we as addicts and/or alcoholics don't find something else to give us the same ease and comfort that drugs and alcohol gave us, we will use again. Many others and I have discovered that in a spiritual awakening through a 12-Step program. I have been through some ups and downs in my recovery. But because God and the 12 Steps are the most important part of my life, I have walked through it all.

If there is one thing that I can say about my life today, it is that I feel gratitude on a daily basis that is directly contingent upon my work with the sick and suffering addicts I meet. For many like me, that gratitude is not hard to find. I wake up every morning in a home that my wife and I own, next to the most beautiful spiritual woman in the world. I walk out of my room, and my dogs Milo and Lilly, are two steps behind me. I walk them to the sliding door and let them out to take care of their business. I put on a cup of coffee, do some morning meditation (I am still practicing this), kiss the woman I love goodbye, and head out to a business we own. I end the day at the sober homes with guys who were just like me a few years ago. If I can't find gratitude in that, I am not looking! In early 2003, I was walking the streets of Baltimore, shooting heroin every few hours, sleeping in an abandoned row house, and wanting to die every day.

My wife and I have witnessed so many blessing from these homes. We have gone to weddings and graduations and have seen guys start families. We have actually done the flowers for a few guys who have gone through the house. Let me just say that being at a wedding and seeing a guy dancing with his mother and smiling brings tears to my eyes, knowing that a few years back he walked into our sober home scared and beaten down and his mom was scared he was going to die. Now, they are dancing at his wedding—with three years sober. That is good stuff, people!

My life is a gift, and I intend to not take it for granted and to do whatever God allows me to do to pass this gift on to others.

Part 5

The Ripple Effect Comes Full Circle

The Triangle Recovery Club

At this point in my story, it is only natural to bring up the Triangle Recovery Club. But let me digress for a minute. The ripple effect that my book is named after has, at this point in my life, truly come full circle. By that I mean that in the present times, I am starting to see how my story and my life transformation is helping to make a positive impact on others. Like a drop of water in a pond, which creates a symmetrical, circular ripple effect, my recovery experience has expanded in a ripple effect to embrace others in the community who sincerely want to experience the same kind of recovery from addiction.

I have a great interest in serving as a mentor to others who have walked in the same shoes in which I have traveled, while on the difficult road to recovery. It is my greatest passion to help others who are struggling with addiction of any kind, to help them heal and feel hope again. The Triangle Recovery Club, which I was instrumental in founding, offered its first meeting in September of 2014. The Triangle Recovery Club is a gathering place, that is safe and welcoming for people with all types of addictions, and it is based in Westminster, MD.

The path towards starting the Triangle Recovery Club was long and winding, and it took some time to unfold. The seed of the idea to open a recovery club was planted in the basement of a local church, thanks to a dedicated parish priest who had compassion for those with addiction, and a few people who were hungry and thirsty for successful recovery.

The priest, Father Farmer, wanted to start a heroin "help meeting" at his Westminster church. He envisioned a kind of 12-Step meeting created specifically for heroin addicts. He contacted Deputy State's Attorney Ned Coyne, whom he knew from the parish. Ned approached me and requested that I help to give wings to the idea so that it could get off the ground. This request was the seed for what eventually became the Triangle Recovery Club.

The history behind how it all happened is interesting. I did some research and found that there was a 12-Step program for heroin addicts that started in 2003 in Phoenix, AZ, ironically enough, the same year that I got sober. I reached out to them and asked for a start-up kit. We had a small room in the church where we had our first informal meeting with six guys from the Joey V. and Stonewall sober homes, also named Weber Sober Homes. Within a month, we had 15 participants, and within six months, we had 35 people. The gathering was growing in numbers.

I was probably the logical choice of who would start the "help meeting" that was related to heroin addiction. I was happy to assist with this budding idea of creating a gathering for people addicted to heroin, because I was already doing a lot of educational and awareness-raising activities in the community. I was already working with the local health department in the form of outreach. I was speaking at the local alternative education school for troubled youth. I would speak with the students weekly, about the dangers of drug use and the poor choices I had made. The kids would openly ask questions about why I started using drugs, whether my parents used too, how I decided to quit, and many more insightful wonderings. The outreach work I did was often poignant, as some of those kids I talked with have ended up in the court system, in jail or buried in their graves after overdosing. How sad.

My message also resonated with parents with whom I spoke at the library and other public venues. I offered special insight into parenting a child with addiction because my own daughter and son struggled with addiction.

When I talked with Father from the church, I felt honored, yet unsure. At the time, I was sober for ten years. It was an honor to have the respect of Ned, from the State's Attorney's office, and I felt honored to be asked. However, I was a bit unsure of how I could contribute to launch a gathering just for people addicted to heroin because my knowledge base centered around meetings for alcohol and other drugs. At the beginning of the conversation between me and Father, I was not aware of the existence of the kind of program he was seeking. I actually found out about the Arizona Heroin Anonymous program by searching Facebook.

The premise behind that first church basement meeting is similar to the premise behind most 12-Step meetings: to get people into a relationship with a higher power, and for me, that's God. The other purpose behind this meeting is to reach people early with guidance about the road to recovery. Many young people came to the meeting thinking they were still going to drink socially, because maybe they weren't addicts, after all. They thought that if their issue is heroin, well, what the hell about anything else. They didn't realize that with opiate addiction, the dark side is about any other substance that creates addiction, so they were not "home free." And the problem is that now, communities are losing folks because of fentanyl in drugs.

How did we attract participants to those early meetings? Well, many of the attendees were from the Weber sober homes. They already had a camaraderie with each other. In addition, the health department placed flyers around, and I communicated with the probation office and with the drug court about the meetings. The idea was a perfect fit for the Westminster community and it took off like wildfire. Although some church parishioners disagreed with the idea of holding meetings there, Father continued to believe in the idea, as he was persistent in setting out to work with me and allowed us to continue. He was very happy with the outcome.

I am proud to say that Heroin Anonymous that was started in Westminster was the first such meeting in Maryland. Many are still active in Heroin Anonymous. The effort has really grown, to include more younger folks. Heroin Anonymous has been an antidote to the problems faced by our youth, who as early as 17 or 18 years old, may have already overdosed two or three times. They may have been in two or three rehabs and have definitely hit rock bottom because of heroin. They enter the meetings to talk and to hear stories of success from our people in recovery, folks like myself. In our former lives, we've been running from the police, on probation, unemployable and getting no trust from anyone. We have shared how far down we really were. We show them, through our real- life stories, how they can get out of the downward spiral because we have been clean and sober for a longer time than these kids have even been alive.

Heroin is a deceiving temptation. It has changed enormously since I was a kid, when heroin was something that rock stars did. It was not prevalent on the community level. In the 1990's, as a result of opioid addiction to painkillers, an epidemic grew that almost popularized heroin. The perfect storm was in place for heroin to make its way into the suburbs. Now kids go to a party, with a beer bong, a joint and a bag of fentanyl. Opioids are easily accessible from bathroom medicine cabinets, kids see their friends using, and the drugs are affordable. Kids think they're having fun with these drugs and unfortunately, the lack of parenting and lack of direction I see so much of doesn't help.

The prevalence of fentanyl is another scary story. Around 2014- 2015, fentanyl started taking off as a synthetic opioid that people were mixing with heroin. This created a potency that is 50 times stronger than heroin alone. It was killing people, and still does. Back then, we were starting to see a lot of overdoses and we found that this new drug from overseas was quite cheaper, and stronger, and even more attractive. We were losing youth faster than they could dip their toes into making a fresh start. They had no chance. It all continues to be a problem today, believe me. I see the problem firsthand in the community. People can get a kilo of heroin for $40,000 to $50,000 versus getting a kilo of fentanyl for $2,500. That's a huge difference.

The facts are hard to take and even depressing. But hope is stronger than the strongest drug, in my opinion. It seems that helping others has been my destiny, and that destiny has paved the way for my role in the recovery movement. As you know, I always had ideas to help people out, and no idea was more pressing than my wish to open a recovery club. What does a recovery club offer? Well, the one I really wanted to start in Westminster was modeled after a place in Baltimore City called Stepping Stones, which was three blocks down from the sober living home that I lived in when I embraced sobriety in 2003. Stepping Stones had coffee and snacks, light breakfast and lunch, and individual rooms to hold different 12-Step meetings like Narcotics Anonymous, Al Anon and others. People in recovery could hang out 24/7. I really loved that place and it saved my life, when I didn't have a place to go in my early recovery.

I was very motivated between 2010 and 2013 to find a place to start a local recovery club. I mentioned the idea to my wife, Kathy, who was thinking, "here we go again!" I know she was thinking we just got the sober houses to a point where they didn't drain us monthly and now you want to open a recovery club? I tell this story to this day, but I must say that she supports me completely because she knows how important the recovery community is to me.

When I found what seemed like a great location, everybody shot me down. There is a huge stigma surrounding addiction, and frankly, there was little to no interest among property owners to get involved.

But my luck did turn around. If God is in it, then you can do it. Believe that! On Wednesday nights, we were having a 12-Step meeting in the backyard of the Joey V. house. A neighbor who lived near the sober house noticed how large the group was getting. I told the neighbor that I wanted a bigger place. He gave me the name of the owner of the building, where I actually was able to rent space and provide a formal place for a new recovery club in Westminster. Around Memorial Day, 2013, I met with the owner of the building. I explained what a recovery club is, though he didn't seem to understand, but he said YES! I was floored because I had tried over and over to ask around for a place. Most people looked at me like I had three heads. This guy actually looked at me like I had a light bulb over my head, with my bright idea. I was truthful with him when I said that we have meetings during all hours for people who are recovering from drug and alcohol addictions. Unlike other people to whom I spoke, the walls did not go up with this guy, and he did not shut the door.

Shortly thereafter, I started getting the space ready for meetings. The first meeting was in September, 2013. It's amazing that Two North Court street is now filled with people who are maintaining recovery and who are beautiful, living, responsible human beings.

I called the meeting location Triangle Recovery Club because a triangle is a symbol of recovery. The bottom part of the triangle signifies recovery. The left side is about unity and the right side is for service. The Triangle Recovery Club is not limited to Alcoholics Anonymous meetings, but includes all forms of 12-Step programs, such as Heroin Anonymous, Al-Anon, Narcotics Anonymous, Gambler's Anonymous, and Eating Disorders Anonymous.

The address of Triangle Recovery Club is Two North Court Street, Westminster, MD., 21157. Ironically enough, the local jail is right down at the end of the street at 100 North Court Street. So, if a person attends Two North Court Street (recovery club) they can stay out of 100 North Court Street (jail).

After the lease price was set, and I agreed to the terms, I talked with Kathy. I told her that we needed some money for the deposits. She, being the smart accountant, said, "Tim, you need to figure out another way to get the money." My wife was my sounding board, and we are a good fit in this way.

I said to myself: "I am going to try a fundraiser for a club house on Facebook." I was nervous, because I wondered, what if no one was interested. I was already kind of committed. As seen in my previous stories, I have been known to put the cart before the horse.

I posted the site on Facebook for a Triangle Recovery Club fundraiser to help open the club. I swear, in five minutes, a $500 contribution came in! Yes, that was in five minutes! By week's end, we had raised $6,000 to pay for the first six months of the lease for the club. Another issue I had to overcome (and quite honestly, still do) is the traditions of specific 12-Step programs, or the lack of understanding of them.

By that I mean, I was bashed and criticized to no end about taking money in to open a club house. I get the confusion. Programs that follow 12-Steps are self-supporting and decline outside contributions. True. But a lot of people thought I was asking for money for a specific fellowship. It was just misinformation. This is not a fellowship. This is a building that houses those fellowships and there is nothing wrong with getting money for a place that "houses" 12-Step meetings. Again, there's a lack of understanding. If I explained this once, I have explained it 1,000 times. Churches house meetings and do plenty of fundraisers to keep the doors open. We are no different.

I decided early on that to be successful, we would need to be run by a Board, not by me. First order of business—pick a Board. After many talks with the people who started the Alano Club and Serenity Center in Columbia, MD., I set out to pick members and start some bylaws. I picked people with the same community vision, and people with related skills and expertise for running a nonprofit organization. Some individuals were asked to be in charge of events and cookouts, and others were working on the "unity" part of recovery.

In September, 2014, the Board was in place and so were the first set of bylaws. When I say that we are a team of Board members, I mean that we are a team! We started hashing out meeting times and terms of positions. Soon enough, we were in full operation. As an update, while I started out as president, and spent a few years as ex-officio, I recently resigned from the board in order to open the door for new people to start their own ripple effect. I am still a member of the club and will continue to attend meetings as a part of my recovery.

The club has had many supporters through the years, but the one that has, quite honestly, kept us afloat is the Carroll County Health Department, through a recovery grant for club houses. Without their support, we would not have made it. A huge thank you to Sue Doyle and Cathy Baker.

Today, the club house is the place that houses 22, 12-Step meetings a week—every day of the week—and has a section for activities and events with pinball, air hockey, foosball, and a pool table.

On any given night of the week, you can see people outside of the club, laughing and "fellowshipping" before and after their meetings. I have seen many people walk through those doors broken, beaten and hopeless. Eventually, they smile, and life starts to have true meaning and purpose. It is a beautiful thing.

What has been the impact of the club on its members? Well, hundreds, if not more, people have found recovery through the Triangle

Recovery Club. Some have been mandated to attend by the court system. Others have been told by family members that they need to straighten up.

Members walk in to the club, are welcomed, and they start to engage in the process of recovery. Their lives have actually changed. A little story…I got my license to officiate weddings. People who started their journeys at the club, in some instances, developed relationships. I officiated some of those weddings. They have come full circle, from addiction, to recovery, to new and lasting relationships.

The Triangle Recovery Club is one of the staples of Westminster recovery. It's the hub of the recovery community in Westminster. I absolutely love the place. When I stand outside before or after a 12-Step meeting, I can see literally 50 to 55 people standing outside, having a great time. Or when I sit in on a meeting and hear that someone overdosed and lived to tell about it as a newly-recovered person, my eyes well up with tears of joy that I had a part in this.

The Triangle Recovery Club furnishes a clean, safe facility and environment. Additional support is offered by providing coffee, organizing recovery events and conducting other 12-Step activities. Each group can hold a meeting here, with a percentage of the collection going to the club for rent, coffee and house supplies, and a percentage going to the group, so that smaller groups can grow.

More importantly, the club is a way for me to be a conduit to serve others so that they may form a collective group of people who support each other along the path to recovery. What could be more gratifying?

No one tells this success story better than the folks who have turned the corner on addiction. One mother of an addicted daughter wrote on Facebook: "All you want is for your children to be happy. I thank Triangle Recovery Club for showing my daughter the steps to get there!"

Carroll County State's Attorney's Office

n January, 2015, Carroll County, Maryland had a new State's Attorney: Brian DeLeonardo. I personally always thought that he would make a great State's Attorney. He is personable, engaged in the community, and at the forefront of understanding the opioid epidemic in the county. He is very involved in how to address and solve the problem.

I watched his campaign with interest because of his acknowledgement that something had to be done about the opioid crisis. At the time, I was volunteering with the health department and with county advocacy groups. I was actively speaking to youth, parents and the public, and contributing to drug awareness activities. I was known in the community as knowledgeable about the recovery movement, and people contacted me to help them raise the awareness level of addiction in the county.

Our paths crossed often, with Brian meeting people and establishing himself as a strong candidate in the running. Another elected official whom I would see and talk with at public gatherings was Jim DeWees, who was running for election as county sheriff (he was also elected in 2015). These two individuals were both very much in touch with the pulse of what was needed to move the needle in the right direction to combat the epidemic.

I watched with interest how Brian and Jim were proposing creative answers to the challenges. With Brian in particular, I watched the campaign signs going up, the fundraising events being held, and I attended numerous speaking engagements. I was more attentive to this election than I had ever been before to a political race. In my opinion, it turned out that Brian and Jim were both well-suited for the jobs at hand, and as of the writing of this book, they continue to propose innovative solutions to the age-old problem of addiction.

At the time, I was working full-time at the flower shop and also running the sober homes. All of this was happening at a time when I was celebrating 12 years of sobriety. Life was going along well. Life was good.

Let me elaborate more on the professional relationship which I was developing with Brian. He seemed respectful of me and of my work in the recovery community. We had meetings, we had coffee, and these get-togethers always included important conversations about addiction. The fact that I, a former addict, was interacting with someone at this level, was surreal to me. I was very honored.

In addition, getting to know Jim was instrumental in helping me to navigate the advocacy work I was doing at the time. I had the opportunity to meet key law enforcement members who would become supportive of my work in the addiction and recovery efforts in the county.

Brian was elected, and he was sworn in at a ceremony at Carroll Community College. I remember having an invitation to attend. I wore a suit and tie. During a part of his speech, he mentioned my name as someone who is a leader in the community. I am not going to lie—this literally blew me away.

One of the first things that Brian did when he got into office was to plan the First Annual Drug Overdose and Prevention Vigil. Brian developed the event from a seed of an idea into a reality. The idea was to honor people whom we have lost to overdoses. The concept was to give those individuals a face to their names, so to speak. The 32 people who had passed away from overdoses that year were not going to be forgotten. The event was a gathering of community members that was held at St. Johns Church, in the Portico, which ironically, was the same church where Heroin Anonymous had gotten started. For the event, community members submitted pictures of loved ones who had passed away. A video that included those pictures was presented at the start of the event. Brian spoke about how we all make a difference. I was asked to share my own personal story. A local TV personality who was in recovery also gave remarks. About 500 people attended and the room was packed—standing-room only. At the conclusion of the night, everyone had a candle to light in honor of those who overdosed fatally. Everyone circled within the room, and it was, without question, the most healing night of the year, with some families and friends meeting one another for the first time.

That evening, Brian gave me a special message about something I was intently hoping for. A new staff position created within the organization of the State's Attorney's Office was approved by the Board of Carroll County Commissioners. Brian asked me to accept that position. I was thrilled. Of course, I said yes.

Let me tell you more about the position, which I currently hold. It is the Drug Treatment and Education Liaison for the Carroll County State's Attorney's Office. A little background: there was a movement developing among health departments in the state and the country to start peer recovery coaching programs run by people who had once lived in active addiction and were now sober. Brian wanted to use an approach in which he would hire a liaison to serve as a connection between the courts and individuals who were battling substance abuse. There was a clear need for someone to immediately talk with people who had overdosed, before going to the detention center or to court.

They needed someone to be a sounding board about their addiction, and to understand where they were coming from. They needed someone to tell them more about treatment options. As a result, more people began to think about recovery as an option to help them to turn their lives around.

Remember that in 2015, there were 32 fatal overdoses. Now, that number has probably doubled, mainly as a result of the influx of fentanyl into the county. We were trying to get to the point that if people overdosed again, it would not be fatal. We wanted to help people to stay alive. They would still have consequences for their actions, but they could get help, if they wanted it.

Brian talked with me about such a position, during a meeting in his office, and he laid out the vision of the Drug Treatment and Education Liaison job. I was incredibly interested and said so. Brian told me that he first needed to present to the Commissioners for approval. The night of the First Annual Drug Overdose and Prevention Vigil, Brian communicated to me that, yes, the position was approved. I started the job in June, 2015.

When I arrived on the first day to the office, there were some folks whom I knew, and others whom I met for the first time. I had an email address and got my office set up. My duties? They were to assist people with addiction who were entering the court system to navigate resources in the community. I would meet with them personally, ask them if they were in treatment before, talk about withdrawal, then call local inpatient treatment facilities to offer help.

I was on a 24/7 schedule of availability. I was often at the scene of an overdose to share treatment options with people. Although the work can be demanding, there is no other place that I would rather be. By that I mean, my work has its rewards for me. One time, the sheriff's department called about a young woman who was actively using. I helped to get her into treatment. She wanted the help and it worked for her. The reason I mention this young woman is because she is now three years sober. I officiated the wedding for her and her husband, whom I've also been able to help. It's a success story of which I am proud. By serving as a mentor and a compassionate role model, I resonate with these folks. Slowly, one by one, I can see that people in addiction are responding to the help. It's a win/win situation, all around. I am grateful for the support from the State's Attorney's Office, from law enforcement, from the courts system, and from the entire treatment community, which makes it all possible.

The work I do is a source of my employment, of course, but it is also my passion. I spent many years doing advocacy and outreach before this job. I will always find a special place in my heart to help others. That's because helping others is a big part of my personal recovery. Even if this work were not my job, I would still keep doing it. My work helping others is gratifying. My work helping others is inspiring. This work is motivating and gives me great faith in the power of humanity to overcome the problems of addiction. My job is my true calling in life, as my wife reminds me, when she calls me a lucky man. I also love what I do for a living because my work has impact. People with addiction struggle all hours of the day and night. It is my sincerest honor to be there for them as much as humanly possible. I will never relent in the fight to win the battle against addiction.

Stamp Out Heroin

I f there's one thing I've learned in my professional and personal work as part of the recovery movement, it's that there is a small window of opportunity after a non-fatal overdose (and when someone is revived from it) during which they might be willing to accept help, on some level. That's so that they don't find themselves in an overdose situation again—at least we hope so.

If you remember, in 2015, Carroll County recorded 32 fatal overdoses. Numerous more were non-fatal. A non-fatal overdose is a situation in which someone is revived by Naloxone, and he or she has simply lived to see another day. Data captures the incidents in which law enforcement have responded, and the subsequent outcomes.

Although in 2015, the number of non-fatal overdoses was alarming, this number has probably doubled since that year, as many more people are lost, year after year. In our school programs, we bring home the message by asking the number of students to stand up in their assemblies that equals the number of overdoses. This gives a stunning and sobering visual. It's alarming how heroin seems to be just taking over in the community.

It was, and still is, so important to reach out to people in their urgent times of need, during those twilight moments when they are slowly coming out of the overdose, and realizing the magnitude of what just happened. We want very desperately to get them into treatment, but they must want to do so.

I personally overdosed many times. I knew in my heart, that if I reached out right away with a message of getting treatment, people may choose to get help. Or at least to take baby steps towards that goal.

If someone overdoses, and lives, they are scared. I was so scared the first time it happened to me. I was willing to get any help, and to climb the highest mountain for help, because I could not handle the fear that gripped me when I realized what I had just done. But once I experienced multiple overdoses, I started to think, "What's the big deal?" After multiple overdoses, people tend to still want to get high again! I knew I did. And that's the vicious cycle we are trying to help people stop. By the third, fourth, or fifth overdose, it all becomes "part of the game."

There were certainly challenges in reaching people who overdosed, at exactly the right time, with an offer of help. The hospital could not call me or my office after someone arrived in the emergency room— due to privacy regulations. An EMT in an ambulance could not call me. A doctor or nurse in the emergency room could not call me. Law enforcement was keeping records of all overdoses. They were not held to the same regulations, so they could alert me through an email to my office with a police report. Finally, I was able to know who I could reach out to, on the night or day after an overdose. This approach was innovative. It opened doors to new possibilities. And it gave me hope that I could share my personal story of recovery with people who had sunk so low that they could only start to find their way up again.

Just like a business person has a business card with contact information on it, and distributes it in the hopes that people will call, I needed a similar type of communication to distribute. We created the Stamp Out Heroin card. Printed on the card is a simple message:

"Overdose? Tired? Ready for a Change?" And the slogan at the bottom says, "If you are still breathing, there is hope."

Another reason that we came up with a card was to reach out to people who were refusing after an overdose. They were refusing to get treatment in those important moments. They were refusing a ride in an ambulance to get hospital care. They were refusing every opportunity to get better.

So, by giving people a simple card with a simple, yet powerful message, a law enforcement officer or other first responder would be giving people something to take home with them. If they changed their minds and wanted help, they had the resources easily available to do so—right in their pockets.

We have given out thousands of Stamp Out Heroin cards over the years. I am both impressed and touched by the response to such a simple idea that can actually help to save lives. I recently had another 500 copies printed. They are hotter than pancakes that are just off the griddle.

Each police jurisdiction, towns, and cities in Carroll County have a supply of them, and so does the Sheriff's department. The overdose reports I receive daily in the morning indicate that cards are being given out frequently.

I have a side story to share now. I was standing outside the Triangle Recovery Club once and I got a call from a girl who had received the Stamp Out Heroin card because she was with her husband when he overdosed. The couple called me the next night to tell me they had the card. Yes, they wanted help. I immediately worked on finding the husband a place for treatment in Baltimore. Now, fast forward to a year later. At that time, I received an email from the man and he said he had been in treatment for a year. He was getting ready to graduate from the program. Wonderfully enough, he also completed a GED. The man invited me to attend his graduation. I did attend, and when I walked through the doors to his ceremony, I saw him come over to me with a huge smile on his face. He gave me a big hug. Then, he smiled again to show me his brand, new beautiful teeth, which his program helped to provide. His beautiful smile, his wife, and his little daughter—they were all that I needed to know that my efforts, and the efforts of all who help people, were worth it. I know that I am not alone in the effort. This man had goals, like wanting to become a peer mentor. He now had the opportunity to do it, to move ahead with life.

Such a success story is not as rare as some may think. A good percentage of people accept the help we offer, but the public may not know about it. There is still a stigma to addiction. And of course, we must respect anonymity. A large number of people who survive non-fatal overdoses actually do turn their lives around. I believe the card has played a role in writing those success stories.

The card has produced ripe fruit, so to speak. By that I mean, it is like a seed that grows and keeps blooming, and sprinkling sweet petals of hope over anyone who is willing to listen. People may be given the card and hold onto it, only to call weeks or months later. It doesn't matter how long it takes, because they eventually decide to make the call. The Stamp Out Heroin card was a smart move and has created proven results. Who knew a little information card could make me so happy?

How did we name the card? Well, in certain geographical areas, bags of heroin are stamped with nicknames so that people know what to call them when they buy them. It seemed only natural to relate to that when we created the card. We are trying to stamp out heroin, very literally. Without question, everyone knows what the card is designed to do.

The telephone number on the card has my work cell phone number and my office number printed on it, so that people can easily reach me. It has always worked out that when I am needed, I can be available to talk to people. Recovery is a 24/7 thing for me. I can take calls late at night or during the day. Many calls come in at reasonable times of the day and it's all working out. I am never too tired to help someone in need.

The responses I get from people who never overdose again after receiving the card are heartwarming. I once received a Facebook message from a young man. He said, "Mr. Weber, I got a Stamp Out Heroin card from you about a year ago. You called me and you gave me some direction. I am graduating from my program in April. Can you please attend?" I was so honored.

The success of the card is partly based on its use and timing. How do we "strike" in the window of time? After an overdose, time is urgent and pressing. Time is ticking. Someone may have gotten sick from the overdose, then be withdrawing. Again, time is ticking. Giving out the card stops and resets the clock so that better things can start to happen to people. There is no delay in contacting me. I can quickly give referrals to other resources and providers. That's the way the card is supposed to work, and it works beautifully.

The support from the sheriff's office and the police departments is incredibly helpful. The relationships we have built with them have facilitated all that we do. The card is like a vehicle that helps to put on the brakes to more overdoses. I know people in law enforcement and they know me. And together, we are like a well-oiled machine. I also know many people in the community who are battling addiction, which makes them more familiar with how this all works, and more open to the process.

The Stamp Out Heroin card has now taken on a life of its own. It's almost a movement, because everybody is working together, for the good of others. The local libraries in the county asked for a supply of cards to hand out. Parents at schools have some. The card helps the community, as a whole, with awareness and education about the signs of addiction, and how to navigate resources. The card is like an umbrella of resources that awaits people after they awake from an overdose, open their eyes, and feel a glimmer of hope.

Windows of opportunity. That is what it is all about. There are many resource providers in the community who also understand that a short "window" must be seized in order to help people. One such community member is Tammy Lofink, co-founder of Rising Above Addiction, a nonprofit organization located in Westminster, Md. Rising Above Addiction raises much-needed funds to help people who need funding for treatment, with the understanding that someone who needs help should be able to get it. Lack of money or other resources should not prevent the treatment process from getting starting. In the next chapter, I share how Tammy and Rising Above Addiction have made such a huge difference in our community.

Rising Above Addiction

There are numerous individuals and groups in the community who are eager to help me in my quest to inspire others to overturn their addictions and achieve recovery.

Tammy Lofink, president of Rising Above Addiction in Westminster, Md., is a wonderful advocate. She and her organization are examples of how working together can combat the rising epidemic of addiction, locally, regionally, and around the world.

Rising Above Addiction raises urgently-needed funds to make treatment possible for those who need and want it. Too often, people do not have medical insurance that covers their treatment. They may not have personal funds, or they may not have families and friends to help financially.

Why should anyone who desperately needs treatment after a non-fatal overdose (or who is generally considering letting go of their addiction) not be able to access treatment because of lack of funds? Rising Above Addiction offers an innovative solution to the age-old problem of not being able to afford help towards recovery.

Tammy's story is both inspiring and poignant. Let me tell you more about Tammy.

In 2014, Tammy's son, Robert Mason Lofink, died unexpectedly. She and her family experienced an unbelievable nightmare. Robert died of a heroin overdose. He was only 18 years old. The crushing emotions which followed were too overwhelming.

Tammy has always been an open person, and her openness can help others in a similar situation. Her family's personal story resonates with people with addiction, who feel lonely in their unexpected loss.

Tammy knows that loss and grieving are a part of life. But the addiction that took Robert never goes away. The rates of overdoses are climbing and too many innocent people are affected. Tammy's heart goes out to anyone who suffers in silence, because she understands. Anyone who wants to walk with her on the path to recovery is welcomed and embraced.

People who hear her story are impacted because Robert has changed the trajectory of people's lives. Tammy believes that people with addiction must find a way to afford treatment.

Rising Above Addiction was co-founded by Tammy and started its important work in 2015, on the one-year anniversary of her son's death. Funds are available for detox and cover deductibles for inpatient treatment. People receive help if they want to go to a sober home. Rising Above Addiction runs two sober homes for women: Reclaiming My Life and Keeping My Serenity. The organization helps to navigate treatment for individuals and refers sources of support for families. Tammy has strong relationships with treatment centers.

She has spoken with legislators and has become a community partner with the local health department and the State's Attorney's office. Increasingly, other organizations are contacting Tammy to find out how they can help.

Tammy's story is now self-published in a new book, which is called Reclaiming My Life. It was released in spring of 2020. Already, many people who have purchased the book are telling Tammy that they appreciate her candor in sharing how she healed her pain. The book is an inspiration to all.

Local writer Sylvia Blair of Blair Copywriting and Communications, LLC worked with Tammy as the co-author, to make the book possible. It's important to say that net proceeds from the book Reclaiming My Life do benefit Rising Above Addiction. I offer Tammy and Sylvia my best wishes in telling people Tammy's story of triumph over tragedy.

I also want to share my feelings about the importance of an organization like Rising Above Addiction in the community.

The fact that Rising Above Addiction is available to help get people into treatment is a huge deal. Many people with whom I deal don't have the financial means for treatment. In order to catch them when they are ready and willing, we don't want funds to hold us back. Now, I can help people after I call Tammy. Her funds help to facilitate treatment right away.

Within the community, Rising Above Addiction holds events to bring recovery and non-recovery supporters to hang out together and get to know one another. Some of the events, like the golf tournament and the run, involve a variety of people mixed together in support. Some people are out of jail and recovering, and then later are participating in an event with law enforcement officers who are volunteering at the event or just enjoying it.

Rising Above Addiction is breaking down walls to stigma so that more people are willing to help out. It's easy to forget how much pain a mother can be in, even though she is strong. In everything that Tammy does, she is breaking barriers to getting treatment for people and doing so in a compassionate way.

I first met Tammy at a community event in support of recovery. I was impressed with her from the beginning. Later, we scheduled a meeting at the State's Attorney's office. Tammy met with me and Brian, and some others, to discuss ways that a nonprofit would help with addiction. The question was: what would be the best method to improve treatment options? Well, she could help with facilitating treatment. At that time one of the biggest obstacles was financial barriers. Now, for the first time, there would be a new option available for people in need.

Tammy is a friend and a great contributor to the community. I so appreciate her ideas, her hard work and her commitment. She is a perfect example of someone who has turned the worst tragedy a parent can experience into triumph for many families in the community who are trying to overcome their own pain.

Family Love

Some of the happiest times in my life are when I am spending time with my children and grandchildren. Although I never thought fatherhood would be one of my strongest talents, and truthfully, I did let my kids down a lot, sobriety has given me the ability to be the absolute best father who I can be.

Let me tell you about my children, their children, and our new baby.

My oldest is Megan, whom I introduced you to earlier. She is now 11 years clean and sober. Megan has a 14-year-old son. He is my oldest grandchild and his name is Nicholas. In October, 2019, Megan married a wonderful man named Kenny, whom she met in recovery. Kenny has two beautiful daughters, who are eight and 12. Abby is eight and Hailey is 12. They are my step-grandchildren.

One of the biggest gifts I had in recovery was to walk my daughter down the aisle and give her away on her wedding day. As I have already mentioned, Megan hated and despised me for many years during my active addiction. Amazingly enough, today we share recovery and life together in a beautiful way.

My son is named Michael and I introduced him to you earlier. He recently celebrated one year of being clean and sober, in August, 2020. Michael is married to a wonderful young lady from Texas, who is named Tondie. You hear a lot of people talking about first-love relationships not working out. I can tell you that Tondie and Michael have been together since they were 13 years old, and are still madly in love. They have two beautiful children who are my granddaughters. Kenzie is five and Michelle is ten.

I have a full family, and it feels really good to have all of them in my life. Who would have known that family would become so dear to me, during all of the years that I was chasing drugs?

When we spend time together, it is literally priceless. We have a good time. We see each other throughout the year. Michael is an HVAC technician, a contractor, and works hard. He makes a good living for his family. It really feels good to have two kids who have turned out to be self-supporting and who are living productive lives.

Michael, as a young person, was never as mad at me as Megan was. My relationship with him was different. I coached Michael for a year or two on a Little League baseball team. He was phenomenal and was an incredible catcher. If I had not been so lost in my addiction, he could have gone on to play college ball and pro ball. I regret that Michael didn't have a father-figure supporting him consistently, because I was not around that much. I wish I had been there for every dream and passion that he had in life. I wasn't able to be that person for Michael. It's fine now, though, and we have talked about it.

My relationship with Megan is really good now. Megan and I actually share the same 12-Step recovery group. We go to meetings together every week—that's pretty cool. We enjoy recovery together in that way, and something like this is not so unusual. I know many other people with similar situations to ours. They and their kids have dealt with active addiction, and now are sharing recovery.

Now, let me introduce you to Declan, our bouncing baby boy. Yes, we do have a new baby that has been the joy of our lives. When Kathy and I got married in 2005, I was 37 years old, and I had already had a vasectomy. I had no intention of starting another family, at that point. Would I even live to see age 40?

After we got married, we talked about having kids. In today's world, with medical advances, we knew we could get help.

Six months after our wedding, I had the vasectomy reversed, and everything was fine. Around that same time, my daughter Megan was pregnant with Nicholas. Kathy wanted to wait to get pregnant until after Megan would give birth. So, we waited to conceive. Then, Megan got sick. We put things off for a little while, because so much was going on all around us.

The time came for us to start trying, but it was not working out. After one year of trying naturally, we went back to the doctor. He said it's not impossible to conceive after a vasectomy reversal, but not as likely as it was before the procedure. He said if nothing happens in six months, Kathy and I should explore other options such as In vitro fertilization (IVF). At first, we thought it was not an option. We even thought about fostering children, and took a class, and even completed application paperwork. I was sober for eight years, but I still had an extensive criminal record from my past. I was honest when filling out the papers about my history. Sadly, they told Kathy and me that my past history disqualified us from becoming foster parents. This news was a gut shock. I was working with 14 guys in sober homes, yet I was not considered responsible? What a disappointment!

We went back to the doctor to try IVF again. In 2015, the insurance I had through my employer made it easier for us to try again because the procedure was covered. We went through five cycles of procedures, but again, nothing worked. It was an agonizing process to wait and see if Kathy got pregnant.

The hardest thing for me was to watch Kathy—who wanted children more than anything else in the world—go through such pain.

I blamed myself, I had mixed emotions, and it was all a strain on our relationship. We decided to stop trying.

We wanted to take the trip of a lifetime to Africa, and put the idea of a baby behind us. Then, we got a call from a fertility doctor about a new procedure that increased the chance for the embryos to implant. It turns out that the difficulty, over all of that time, was implantation. Would we be willing to try again? We were willing to. Unfortunately, it didn't work, once again. It was our last shot with insurance coverage. We talked about the trip again, and came to the conclusion that we were not going to have our own children.

Then one year later, we talked and prayed. We told one another that we would give this thing one more shot, because if we didn't, we would wonder for the rest of our lives if we did the right thing. We had a different doctor. We started shots, an embryo implanted, and this time, something just felt different to me. After a two-week wait, Kathy called me up at work. I knew she was calling to say that she was pregnant. It was just a feeling that I had. That feeling turned out to be right—Kathy was pregnant! Yay!

Then the journey of our baby boy began—visits to make sure everything was okay, and everything you could imagine to make sure this baby would be healthy. It was a perfect pregnancy and Kathy worked at her job until she had Declan, with no major issues. Kathy was scheduled to have a planned C-section because the baby was in a breech position at the end of the pregnancy. The C-section was planned for December 13, 2019. On December 12, 2019, around 8 a.m., Kathy's water broke, and we rushed around and got things ready to drive her to the hospital. By 12:43 p.m. that day, Declan was born.

From the moment he was born, Declan has been a complete blessing to us. He slept through the night right away. Recently, we took Declan to the beach for the first time. He loved the water, and he loved playing with our dogs Lily and Milo.

Because of the COVID-19 pandemic, I was working remotely from home, and Kathy was working at the flower shop. Declan had been with one or both of us all of the time. He had not spent a day in a child care setting, thanks to our time at home together.

Fatherhood is really different this time around. One thing I have learned more than anything is that the most important gift we have to give is our time and attention. So that's what he gets, and a lot of it. When Declan is around, he gets my undivided attention, and I'm not on the phone or reading email. I've been aware of not getting distracted by my work. We have a set routine. I give Declan a bath every night, put him in pajamas, then hand him off to Kathy to read a book, say prayers, and give him a bottle. He sleeps for 12 hours, believe it or not!

Kathy and I take turns with who gets up early with him. She and I are really good partners, and it works out really well. We're already talking about where we want him to go to school. This time around, I have more financial means that I had with Megan and Michael. Kathy went to private school and I went to public school, so we know all of the ins and outs of the decision.

For now, we are savoring every time he crawls, or rolls over, or gives us a high-five. It was so much fun to see him eat baby food from a spoon for the first time. All of his "firsts" are fun.

What are my hopes and dreams for Declan? I hope that he will win the green jacket at the Masters Tournament and think I helped him along the way (I will teach him to golf!). But seriously, I know that he will grow up with two loving parents and will be surrounded by a big, loving family. He will know how much we love him. He will know how much God loves him. I know that he will pass this love on to his own children when that time comes.

I want Declan to be happy, whatever he does. My life was different when my older kids were growing up, and I want Declan's story to be happier. Declan will know that he has two parents who love each other. Declan was twelve years in the making. He will be forever in my heart and in the heart of his mother. I am truly a lucky man now that I am clean and sober.

Reflections

Looking back, my life has been a wild rollercoaster ride with many interesting—even dangerous—twists and turns. I started out with a difficult home life as a youth, yet grew up like most of my friends, with an interest in sports and socializing. I was introduced to drugs and fell in love with them, and eventually, I became addicted. That drug addiction cost me my family, my job, and my sanity.

I ended up in the gutter, with no place to live, no hope, and no place to turn. When I finally got tired of this kind of life—which would ultimately kill me—I also got tired of the looks of disappointment and disgust in the faces of the family and friends who meant so much to me. I was on my last leg, and so were they. Support was nowhere to be found, and I felt desperately alone.

As you know, this story does have a happy ending. Today, my life is successful, happy and overflowing with supportive family and friends. I am sober and more than that, I am committed to a sober lifestyle. I work for an important government agency that allows me to reach out to people who are in active addiction and help them towards recovery. I am a proud dad and grandad. I have a loving wife. And I am a community activist who spends countless hours reaching out with my personal story to hopefully impact the lives of others.

No matter how far down drugs and alcohol can take you, as long as you are willing to accept help, follow direction and be open-minded, you can recover from what seems to be hopeless. A lot of people don't know a lot of my story. People do not realize that I did not turn things around till I was 37 years old. It doesn't matter how old you are, you can still turn your life around. I am now finishing my bachelor's degree in business in my 50's. I am doing this for personal fulfillment and to perhaps advance my career, but it's been a challenge. Remember, I spent decades experiencing personal destruction and I missed learning the everyday things that most people know in life. I didn't know much about politics or current events. All I knew was how to hustle on the street to get high. I was very good at adapting to any situation to help me get high. The point is that it doesn't matter how far down you fall. You can still pull yourself out of a dark situation and turn your life around. Today I have an incredible life. I can pay all my bills. I have a nice home. Best of all, I have a deep sense of accomplishment in my heart and mind.

Don't get me wrong. Staying sober over time has its obstacles. You must stay vigilant throughout the recovery process in order not to relapse. Recovery must be the most important thing in your life. If it is not, you risk losing everything you've gained. I see this happen all too often to well-meaning and dedicated people.

I don't want to sound depressing, but the facts are the facts. Addiction is something that is going to be around forever because it's a chronic condition. It's not going to go away, and in my opinion, addiction is getting worse. The demand for illegal drugs is high and so is the supply. Malicious people are creating new drugs that can fly under the radar of drug tests. These drugs are also cheaper. People can even unknowingly begin a harmful relationship with drugs, like when they take pills to stay awake longer, and cannot stop. The case for prevention of addiction has never been stronger and more urgent than it is today.

Looking back on a life that spiraled downward and somehow bounced back to normalcy makes me eternally grateful for the gains which I have made. I'm literally grateful for every breath I take. I shouldn't be alive after what I went through. I am most grateful for people who influenced me in my life, people like Isiah Robertson. The Isaiah House Treatment Center, and Isiah's personal relationship with God, introduced me to the importance of knowing a higher power. I am grateful to Bill Wilson and Dr. Bob, who were also a big reason for my recovery. They showed me another way to live and how to sustain my new lifestyle.

The primary way I stay clean and sober is by helping other people. One day, I hope that my legacy will be that I influenced and helped other people to escape from a living hell into a new and beautiful life. I hope my actions have a ripple effect in the community, which is needed more today than ever. My wish for everyone who attempts to recover from addiction is that they experience much success. I cannot say enough how proud I feel of anyone and everyone who takes that first brave step towards marching out of addiction into a new life of possibilities. I stand ready to encourage, embrace, support and applaud them. The future is bright for all of us.

Acknowledgements

My recovery and this book would not have been possible without all the people who helped along the way.

- First and foremost, I want to thank God for everything.
- My wife, Kathy, who is truly my guardian angel. I love you so much, babe. Thank you for believing in me. You are truly the most spiritual, loving, and caring person I know.
- My two kids, Megan and Michael, who sadly, had to grow up without a father most of their lives. I love you both more than you may ever know. I will always be here for you.
- Our beautiful miracle son, whose name is Declan.
- My dad and stepmom (Arlene). I hope all the years of pain I have caused you both will be replaced with years of joy and happiness. I love you both very much. Thank you for never giving up on me.
- My mom, Miriam, I hope you are looking down on me and saying, "That's my Timothy Turtle." I really miss you and the years I lost with you.
- My brothers, Pat and Mike, with whom I fought growing up. I look forward to every second we spend together today, especially on the golf course. I love the both of you so much. Thank you for all you have done for me through the years.

- My grandchildren, Nicholas, Michelle, and Kenzie, what a blessing you are. I hope you only know the Papa you know today, clean and sober.

- My in-laws, Mike and Katie. I am so blessed to have married into a family that is so full of love. I will never forget how you two never made me feel less than, even when I was.

- Mike, Karen, and Steve, I thank you all for accepting me and forgiving me for the past and giving me a chance to show you I would be good to your little Roo. Steve, I miss you in death more than you know. Just love…

- Isiah, thanks for introducing me to God. Thank you for helping me to create the first circle in my very own ripple effect.

- George Butler, thanks for introducing me to everyone in Carroll County, especially to Linda Auerback.

- My sponsor, Spence. Thank you for being the example to follow on my journey of recovery. You have helped me more than you will ever know.

- The Storches. I love you all. You were my home away from home.

- Timmy, my house manager at the Linwood House. Thank you for all your support.

- All my friends of Bill W., thanks for telling me to "keep coming back." You know who you are!

- Jim C. I value our friendship so much and thank your for introducing me to George from the Choices program. It has opened so many doors.

- George, Tracy, and Anne-Marie from Choices. I look forward to every month we spend together.

- Mandy, thank you for all the hard work you do to make our business a success.

- My dog, Munchkin, who when he was alive, was the coolest dog. Now, our dogs Milo and Lily fill our home with laughter and love.
- Keith S., house manager and new president of Weber Sober Homes.
- All the residents—past and present—of Weber Sober Homes.
- A special thank you to Sylvia Blair, owner of Blair Copywriting and Communications, LLC, for her writing and editing assistance in preparing this third edition of my book.

My mother Miriam Weber

My first fight at 12 years old

Me, 1983 Centennial High School Lacrosse

Me and State's Attorney Brian DeLeonardo

Me receiving a citation from Maryland Governor Larry Hogan
for work in the field of addiction and prevention

My daughter on her wedding day

My son and granddaughter Michelle

Me and Kathy on our wedding day

Tim, Kathy, and Declan Weber

The Weber Boys – Dad, Mike, Tim, & Pat

Michelle, Tim & Kenzie (granddaughters)

Grandson Nicholas following in granddads footstep

About the Author

Tim, Kathy, and Declan Weber

Tim Weber resides in Westminster, Maryland with his wife Kathy. Together, they own and operate Cattails Country Florist, Inc. in Woodbine, Maryland. He is the father of two grown children, Megan and Michael, and is a grandfather. He is also the proud daddy of Declan. Tim and his wife Kathy feel so blessed to be the mommy and daddy of the miracle baby.

Tim is the Drug Treatment and Education Liaison for the State's Attorney's Office in Carroll County, Maryland. He is on the Carroll County Behavioral Health and Addictions Planning Committee,

Opioid Response team, LEAD, and is the founding board member of the Triangle Recovery Club.

Tim also founded the Weber Addiction Group and Weber Sober Homes.

He is the published author of *Gutters and Roses, With Notes from a Sober Home.*

Tim is certified through the Maryland Association of Prevention Professionals and Advocates, as a prevention specialist, and is completing his bachelor's degree in business. He was the 2011 Risky Business Award winner for substance abuse prevention, and the DEA's Light of Hope Award winner in 2014. In 2017, he received a governor's citation for his work in the field of prevention and treatment for substance abuse disorders. Most importantly, he is in long-term recovery since 2003, from a substance use disorder.